SEE & EXPLORE LIBRARY

THE BODY
and HOW IT WORKS

Written by
Steve Parker

Illustrated by
Giovanni Caselli
Giuliano Fornari
Sergio

DORLING KINDERSLEY, INC.

NEW YORK

DK

A DORLING KINDERSLEY BOOK

Editor Angela Wilkes
U.S. editor B. Alison Weir
Art editor Roger Priddy

Editorial director Jackie Douglas
Art director Roger Bristow

Editorial consultant Dr. Frances Williams

10 9 8 7 6 5 4 3 2 1

Dorling Kindersley, Inc., 232 Madison Avenue
New York, New York 10016

Library of Congress Cataloging-in-Publication Data
Caselli, Giovanni, 1939-
The Human Body; and how it works / Giovanni Caselli : contributing
illustrators, Giuliano Fornari, Sergio - 2nd American edition.
p. cm. - (See & Explore library) Includes index.
Summary: Examines the systems and parts of the human body and how
they work, including the skin, blood, bones, lungs, and heart.
ISBN 1-879431-95-5 (trade)
ISBN 1-879431-96-3 (lib. bdg.)
1. Human physiology - Juvenile literature. 2. Body, Human - Juvenile
literature. [1. Body, Human. 2. Human physiology.]
I. Fornari, Giuliano, ill. II. Sergio, ill. III Title. IV Series.
[QP37.C33 1992]   91-58203
                                                     CIP AC

Phototypeset by SX Composing, Essex
Reproduced in Singapore by Colourscan
Printed in Spain by Artes Graficas. Toledo S.A.
D.L.TO:33-1992

CONTENTS

THE BODY MACHINE

Look at a machine such as an airplane. Like all other machines, an airplane has many different parts, parts that need to work properly so that it can do its job.

You can look at animals in the same way. You will notice how each part of an animal's body is made for a certain job. A giraffe has a long neck so that it can eat leaves that other animals cannot reach. A lion has sharp teeth for biting and tearing up prey.

Now look at your own body. You can see that, just like a piece of machinery or a part of an animal, each part of your body has a different job to do. Why do you have ears? Why are your legs and fingers shaped the way they are? Try to answer these questions for yourself and then see if you are right.

This book explores the main areas of the body and the important parts that fit inside each area. But before looking at areas like the head, chest, back, and so on, take a look inside a complete human body, shown in one extended picture over this and the next three pages.

Your central control room
Your brain is the most important part of your body. Every moment of your life, your brain is either sending out messages or receiving them back from the rest of your body. *More about your brain on pages 24-27.*

Listening to sounds
Your ears collect sounds from the air around you. The sound travels deep into your ears to your brain, which tells you what you are hearing. Ears also help you to keep your balance. *More about ears on pages 32-33.*

Sending blood around
Almost in the middle of your chest is a very special muscle. This muscle, called your heart, pumps your blood to your lungs and to all the other parts of your body. *More about the heart on pages 40-41.*

Holding on to things

Your arm is like a pole extending to your hand so that you can reach out. Your hand is an extremely useful part of your body. It is made up of a flat palm and five fingers. By bending your fingers or holding them against your palm, you can grasp objects, use tools, push things away, or pull things toward you. *More on arms and hands on pages 42-43.*

What's inside your body?

The picture below, of the back of a person's body, shows how well designed the human body is. Many parts of the body are delicate, so the most important parts are protected by strong bones. The brain, the body's control center, is protected by the skull. Bones in the back and chest protect the heart and the lungs. The hip bone protects other important parts.

Your body's transportation system

The red liquid that flows around your body is blood. Blood is very important because it carries food and oxygen from one part of your body to another. Your heart pumps your blood through your body along tubes called arteries. Blood travels back to your heart through narrower tubes called veins. *More about blood on pages 16-17.*

Your body's framework

Almost all of the hard parts inside your body are bones. You have about 200 bones in your body, and when they all fit together they make up your skeleton. Bones give your body a strong frame, protect your insides, and allow you to move. *More about bones on pages 18-21.*

Breathing in air

A lot of space inside your chest is taken up by two spongy bags called lungs. When you breathe in, air goes down into your lungs so that they fill up like balloons. Some of the air goes to other parts of your body. What's left is pushed out of your lungs when you breathe out. *More about lungs on pages 38-39.*

How food leaves your body

Ingested food is used to make you grow or to give you energy. After food leaves your stomach, it travels through a long tube called your intestine. Any food still left by the time it reaches the end of the tube leaves your body as waste. *More about your digestive system on pages 46-49.*

Eating, tasting, and talking
Your mouth helps you do many things. You take food in through your lips, and bite and chew it with your teeth. Your tongue helps your food go down your throat, and also tells you whether the food has a nice or nasty taste. Your lips, teeth, and tongue also help you speak. *More about your mouth on pages 34-35.*

Seeing and watching
Your eyes give you pictures of the world around you. You can see only when it is light because light is needed to make a picture on the back of your eyeballs. The picture then travels to your brain, which tells you what you are seeing. *More about eyes on pages 30-31.*

Where food goes
Your stomach is a kind of stretchy bag where the food you eat is broken up. This makes it easier for the food to travel to the rest of your body. *More about the stomach on pages 46-47.*

Where babies grow
Inside every girl's body is a small, hollow bag called a womb. When she is an adult, this is where a new baby may grow before it is born. *More about how babies grow on pages 50-53.*

Inside the legs and feet
In the picture above, you can see inside the lower part of a human body.

6

The front of a female's body
The picture on the left shows what the front of a girl's body would look like if you could see inside her. Many of the most important parts of the body can be seen only from the front.

Carrying messages around
In every part of your body, you have tiny connecting "wires" called nerves. Some nerves carry messages to your brain, telling it what the rest of your body is feeling. Other nerves take orders from your brain to your muscles, telling them when to move. *More about nerves on pages 12-13.*

A protective covering
Your entire body is covered by skin. Skin not only helps to protect your insides from being hurt or being infected, but also keeps your body from getting too hot or too cold. *More about skin on pages 8-11.*

Walking around
In order to carry your heavy body while you walk, run, and jump, your legs must have strong muscles and bones. Your feet push at the ground as you walk and help you to balance. *More about legs and feet on pages 60-61.*

How you move
Muscles are the parts inside your body that make you move. They are joined to your bones. All muscles are under orders from your brain. When your brain tells them to work, they do so by pulling a bone or bending or straightening a joint. *More about muscles on pages 14-15.*

Facts about your body

Your body contains
- 206 bones (in an adult)
- approximately 639 muscles

Of your total body weight
- your skin makes up more than 10%
- your muscles make up 40%
- your bones make up 25%
- your brain makes up 2%

Your heart beats
- an average of 70 times a minute
- 100,000 times a day without rest throughout your life

When you were born, you were probably
- about 28% of your final height if you are a boy
- about 30% of your final height if you are a girl

Your brain
- has 10 million nerve cells, and each nerve cell has a potential 25,000 interconnections with other nerve cells
- is made up of 80% water

Your entire body
- is about 70% water

YOUR SKIN

When you look at your body, the largest organ you can see is skin. It is your all-purpose covering. It is waterproof – in both directions. It keeps water out and, more important, it keeps water in. Your insides have to be kept moist and bathed in body fluids, or they would dry out and stop working. (In fact, skin is more water repellent than waterproof. That is, if you stayed in water for too long, your skin would get soggy and begin to "leak.")

Skin is also germproof. It is a tough barrier that keeps harmful microbes out of your body. Most germs get into the body through "holes" in the skin, such as the nose and mouth, or through a cut in the skin. Skin also protects your insides from the sun's harmful ultraviolet rays.

Skin is flexible and supple. As you move, your skin stretches over the parts that bend, then springs back into shape afterward.

Skin does not wear away. It is always replacing itself (*see page 10*). If it is rubbed hard, skin becomes even thicker, in order to resist the wear. This is why people who do heavy work with their hands have hard, thick patches of skin (*called calluses*) on them. If skin is damaged, it is able to repair itself.

Skin does many other jobs. It helps to maintain and regulate your body temperature and it has the sense of touch. (*See pages 10-11.*)

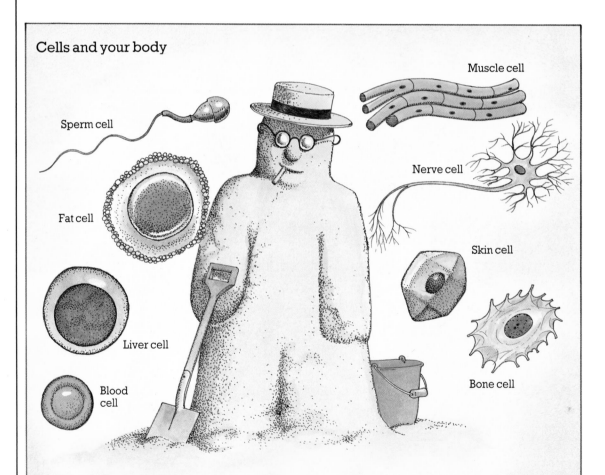

Cells and your body

Sperm cell

Muscle cell

Fat cell

Nerve cell

Liver cell

Skin cell

Blood cell

Bone cell

A sandman is made of tiny grains of sand. In a way, you are like a sandman. Your body is made of tiny parts too, called cells. In your case, however, not all these parts are the same. There are many different kinds of cells in various parts of your body. Some of them are shown above. Each main part, or *organ*, of your body is made of different kinds of cells. The shape of each cell depends on what job it does, and cells are always doing their jobs, making chemicals, or changing one substance into another, or dividing to form new cells. Some cells, like those in your skin and blood, live only for a few weeks. Other cells, such as those in your nerves and bones, may be as old as you are. An average cell is about one-thirtieth of a millimeter across – so small that you can see it only with a microscope. There are about 50,000 million cells of different kinds in your body.

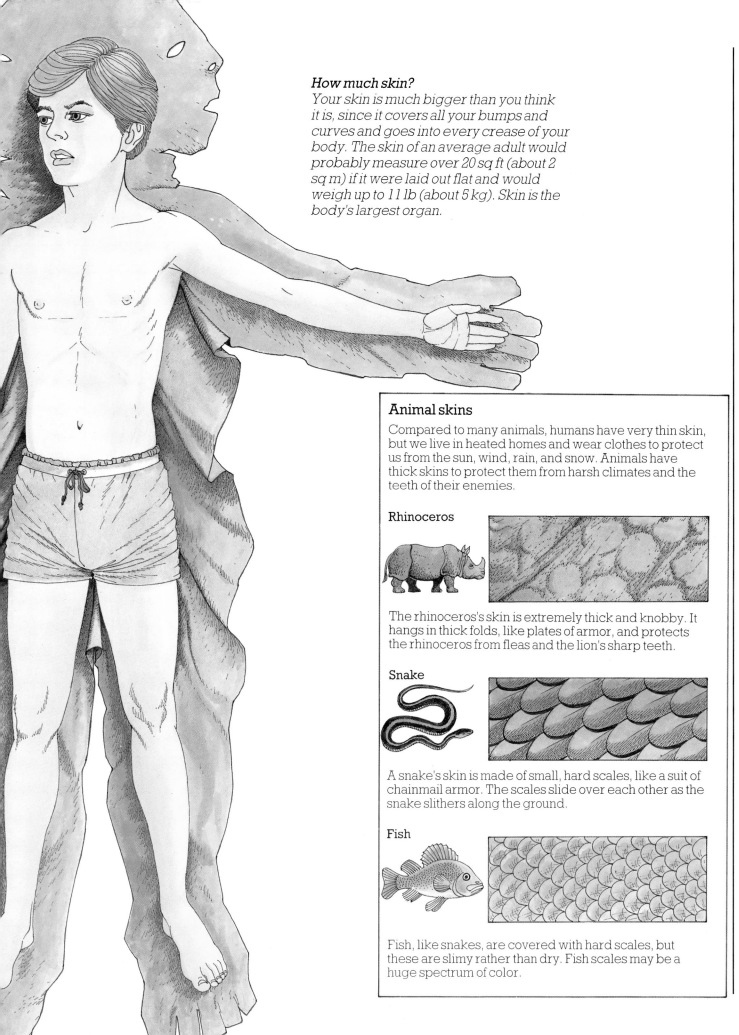

How much skin?
Your skin is much bigger than you think it is, since it covers all your bumps and curves and goes into every crease of your body. The skin of an average adult would probably measure over 20 sq ft (about 2 sq m) if it were laid out flat and would weigh up to 11 lb (about 5 kg). Skin is the body's largest organ.

Animal skins

Compared to many animals, humans have very thin skin, but we live in heated homes and wear clothes to protect us from the sun, wind, rain, and snow. Animals have thick skins to protect them from harsh climates and the teeth of their enemies.

Rhinoceros

The rhinoceros's skin is extremely thick and knobby. It hangs in thick folds, like plates of armor, and protects the rhinoceros from fleas and the lion's sharp teeth.

Snake

A snake's skin is made of small, hard scales, like a suit of chainmail armor. The scales slide over each other as the snake slithers along the ground.

Fish

Fish, like snakes, are covered with hard scales, but these are slimy rather than dry. Fish scales may be a huge spectrum of color.

9

UNDER YOUR SKIN

On the outside, you are "dead." Your hair and the surface of your skin are made of dead cells. But less than a millimeter under the surface of your skin are some of the busiest cells in your body. They are continually dividing to make new layers of skin cells which harden and die, to replace the top layer of skin as it is worn away. Every day, millions of dead skin cells rub off as you wash, dry yourself with a towel, get dressed, and move around. Much of the "dust" in a house is dead skin which has rubbed off people's bodies.

This wearing away happens only in the top part of the skin, which is called the *epidermis*. The epidermis protects the lower layer of your skin, the *dermis*. The dermis is made of a tough, elastic substance that gives skin its stretchiness and springiness. In the dermis are the blood vessels that bring food to your skin; the nerve endings that sense touch, heat, cold, and pain; and the sweat glands and oil glands that help to keep your skin supple and water repellent.

Your skin is not the same all over your body. Your hands have many tiny ridges for a good grip. On the soles of your feet, the skin is very thick, because this is where it wears away the most.

Inside your skin

On most parts of your body, your skin is about one millimeter thick. Under a microscope you can see the two main layers – the epidermis (the top, dark layer) and the dermis. The skin shown here comes from the top of your head, where each hair looks like a tree trunk.

On the surface
The hard, dead cells on your skin's surface lock together like tiles on a roof. As they wear away, more dead cells move up from below.

Making new skin
At the bottom of the epidermis, new skin cells are continuously being made. They thicken, harden, and die as they are pushed up by more new cells.

Muscle

Blood vessels

Color is skin deep
People whose ancestors came from different parts of the world have different-colored skin. All skin contains a coloring called *melanin*. Dark skin contains more of it than fair skin, as melanin protects the skin from damage from too much sun by "shading" the deeper layers of skin. People originating from hot, sunny places have dark skin. Those from cooler places are fair-skinned because they do not need as much protection, but they can get a tan if they spend a lot of time in the sun. Beneath the skin, everyone is the same.

Sensitive skin
Skin is packed with nerve endings. These can detect touch, heat and cold, and pain. (*see page 29*).

Hairy skin
Hairs grow from deep pits in the skin called *follicles*. Hair is made up of dead, hardened cells.

Pore

Fat cells

Keeping cool
Deep in the lower layer of skin are coiled-up tubes called sweat glands. You have about three million of them altogether. They make watery sweat that cools your body.

Staying supple
Waxy and oily substances are made by tiny glands (*sebaceous glands*) near each hair. These "natural oils" prevent your skin from drying out and cracking, and keep it soft and supple.

Temperature control
Your skin helps you to stay at your ideal temperature of 98.6°F. Your brain regulates your temperature by controlling how much blood flows through your skin.

Flushing

When you get too hot, the blood vessels in your skin become wider. More blood flows through them, so you lose more heat and cool down. The extra blood in your skin makes you look pink, or "flushed."

Sweating

Another way of staying cool is by sweating. Watery sweat comes from the skin's sweat glands (see left). As the sweat evaporates, it draws heat from your body to cool it.

Pale skin and shivering

When it's cold, the blood vessels in your skin become narrower. This cuts down the amount of heat lost through your skin and makes you look pale. Your muscles make extra heat by working on their own; this action is called shivering.

YOUR NERVES

Your body is buzzing with electricity. Even when you are asleep, electrical signals are flashing back and forth, as one part of the body signals to another. The amounts of electricity in the signals are tiny – only a fraction of the strength of a telephone signal or even a flashlight battery. But they are strong enough to make your muscles work and to tell you about your surroundings, using your senses. These tiny signals are called nerve impulses.

The "wires" of the body are called nerves. They run in large bundles, like electrical cables, all over your body. Each nerve separates and connects to a certain part. Most nerves run to and from the brain, which is the "control center" of the whole nervous system (*see page 24*).

Nerves are made of cells called *neurons*. A single nerve cell is much thinner than an electrical wire – it is about one-hundredth of a millimeter across. But, like a wire, it can be very long. The nerve cells that go right down to your toes might be over a yard long!

A tunnel of bone

Nerve cells are very delicate. Many types of cells can divide to form new cells when damaged, but a nerve cell cannot. So the body has to protect its nerves. Your brain is in a hard, bony box – your skull. Your spinal cord is in a flexible bony tunnel – your backbone, or spine. To connect to the body, nerves branch off from your spinal cord and run between the bones (*vertebrae*) of your spine.

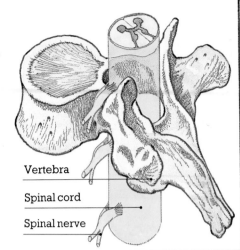

Vertebra

Spinal cord

Spinal nerve

Quicker than thinking

Many nerves connect to the brain, but they also connect directly to other nerves that make muscles move. In the "knee jerk," a tap just below your knee makes your leg jump. This is a *reflex*, a "short circuit," as it bypasses nerves that connect to the brain.

Sending signals

Your nervous system has connections to all the parts of your body. Part of the system runs automatically – keeping your lungs breathing, for instance. Other nerves go into action when you want to do something, such as clench your fist.

Passing on signals

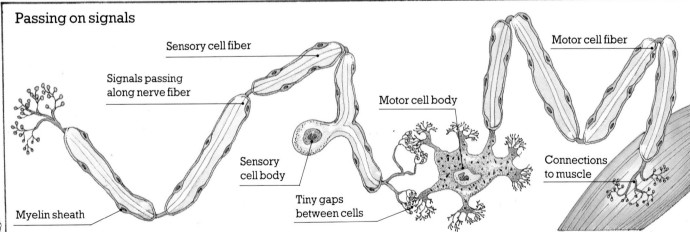

Sensory cell fiber

Signals passing along nerve fiber

Motor cell fiber

Motor cell body

Sensory cell body

Connections to muscle

Tiny gaps between cells

Myelin sheath

Here is the simplest nerve connection imaginable: one sensory cell and one motor cell. Each has a fat cell body and a long, thin extension which is the nerve fiber. Like the plastic covering on a wire, the fiber has a fatty covering called the *myelin sheath*, which insulates it. When the sensory cell detects something, it sends out many signals. They flash along the nerve fiber, protected by the myelin sheath, and jump a tiny gap to the motor cell. They go on to reach the muscle and make it tighten.

Between brain and body
Your spinal cord is a thick bundle of nerves that make the connections between your brain and the rest of your body. From it, 30 pairs of smaller nerve bundles branch off. The spinal cord becomes wider at the top and merges into the lower part of your brain.

In charge of the system
Your brain is a mass of nerve cells which control and coordinate the signals coming in and going out. Its electrical signals can be detected by a machine called an EEG (electroencephalograph). *You can read more about how the brain works on pages 24-27.*

Signals coming in
One set of nerves carries signals to your brain from your eyes, ears, nose, skin, and other sense organs. They are called *sensory* nerves. They tell your brain what is happening around you.

Signals going out
Once your brain has decided what to do, it sends out signals along another set of nerves, the *motor* nerves. These have connections to every one of your muscles. When the tiny electrical impulses arrive, they spread into the muscle and make it tighten.

13

MUSCLES AND MOVEMENTS

Almost half your weight is made up of muscles. They are everywhere – even in your skin, eyes, and heart. Every movement you make, from blinking to leaping through the air, depends on muscles. So do the movements inside your body, such as the beating of your heart and the pushing of food through your intestines. Without muscles, your body would be completely still.

When you tense a muscle it gets shorter and thicker. As it shortens, it pulls whatever it is attached to. For instance, the large muscle in the back of your thigh is fixed at the top to your hipbone and at the bottom of your shin bone, just below your knee. When you shorten this muscle, it pulls your shin and your knee bends.

Muscles can only pull. They cannot push. When you relax the muscle at the back of your thigh it becomes floppy, but it does not push your leg straight again. To do this, you have to tense the muscle at the front of your thigh. This pulls the front of your shin, straightening your leg. Many muscles in your body work like this, in pairs. One pulls a part one way, and the other pulls it back.

How far can you jump?

When you jump through the air you use more than just your leg muscles. Your arms swing back, then up and out to help you balance. Your back straightens, then your head and body bend as you land. All these movements depend on teams of muscles shortening and then relaxing at exactly the right moment.

Taking to the air
As you take off, four sets of muscles are shortening. They straighten your hips, knees, ankles, and even your feet and toes. Muscles that work your toes are in front of your lower leg, connected to your toes by tendons (*see pages 60-61*).

Power for the push-off
First you crouch down. Then you tense the muscles at the front of your thighs and the back of your calves. This straightens your knees and stretches your feet for the jump.

Inside a muscle

A muscle is composed of many thick bundles. Each bundle is made of small, stringy muscle fibers. In turn, each fiber is made of even smaller fibers called fibrils.

There are also tiny nerves in a muscle, which control how much it shortens. And there are plenty of blood vessels, to supply the muscle with the energy it needs to work.

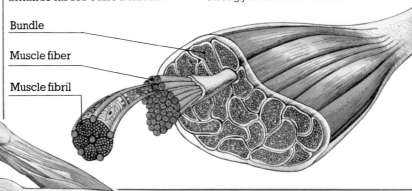

Bundle

Muscle fiber

Muscle fibril

In midair
At the top of your jump, your leg muscles are loose and relaxed, except for small adjustments to keep you balanced. As you come in to land they shorten again, ready to absorb the landing.

When muscles get tired

Most muscles become tired after a while. All through the day, your neck muscles move your head, your jaw muscles open and close your mouth, and your eyelid muscles open your eyes. As you become tired, these muscles relax. Your head nods forward and your eyes close. Soon you are asleep, resting the muscles for tomorrow.

The muscle that never tires

Your heart is made of a special type of muscle called cardiac muscle. When it tightens it squeezes blood out of your heart. This is a heartbeat. Cardiac muscle works all day and all night, never tiring.

Moving on its own

Your intestines and other inside organs are made of "involuntary" muscle. This type of muscle is called involuntary because you can't order it to move when you want to. It works automatically, steadily pushing food through your intestines.

Moving when you want to

Muscles that move your arms, legs, face, head, and body are "voluntary" muscles. This means you can order them to move when you want to. Often you have to concentrate hard on which muscles to use, as when you learn to ride a bicycle and you need to pedal, steer, and balance all at once. When you have had a lot of practice, you can use your voluntary muscles without really thinking.

BLOOD: A TRANSPORTATION SYSTEM

Your eight pints (4.5 liters) of blood contain so many substances and do so many jobs that it is difficult to list them all. The most important thing blood does is supply oxygen and digested food to every part of your body. Also, it takes away waste chemicals to be dealt with by your lungs, liver, and kidneys.

Blood carries many special chemicals around the body. It distributes the hormones that control such things as growth and sexual development. Its clotting chemicals seal cuts in your skin. Its white cells help to fight infection. And it helps to control your body temperature (*see page 11*).

Blood flows out of your heart into tubes called arteries. These divide into branches again and again until they are too small to see. These microscopic tubes, only one-hundredth of a millimeter across are called *capillaries*, and they reach every part of your body. Their walls are so thin that oxygen and other substances can seep through them from the blood into the body tissues. The capillaries join together, become larger, and form veins that take the blood back to your heart.

Watertight vessels
Your main blood vessels, the arteries and veins, are watertight – or rather they are "bloodtight." Blood cannot escape from them. Only when they have divided many times to form capillaries can substances seep out of the blood, into the tissues of your body.

What is blood made of?
Over half of your blood is made up of a watery liquid called *plasma*, which contains dissolved chemicals like salt and food. The rest is cells. Most of them are doughnut-shaped red cells, which carry oxygen. These are small, even for cells; each one is only seven-thousandths of a millimeter across. There are also white cells, which fight infection, and *platelets*, which help blood to clot. In a pinhead-sized drop of blood, there are five million red cells, 10,000 white cells, and 250,000 platelets.

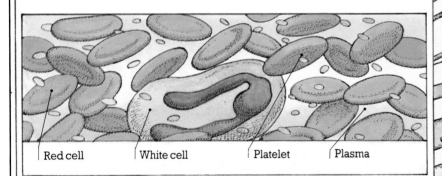

| Red cell | White cell | Platelet | Plasma |

How blood clots
Normally, blood cells cannot escape from their vessels (**1**). If you cut yourself, blood begins to leak out of the broken vessel (**2**). This must be stopped, or your blood could ooze away! Clotting is started by tiny platelets floating among the blood cells. Quickly they begin to stick together (**3**). They form a sticky lump that traps red cells (**4**). Chemicals from the platelets react with chemicals in the blood to make a microscopic net that traps more cells. A blood clot forms (**5**), hardens and seals the cut (**6**).

Delivery and collection
Your blood is a transportation system; it runs a delivery and collection service. Every part of your body needs oxygen (the red carriers in the picture), and blood takes it there along the arteries. Every part of your body makes carbon dioxide and wastes (the blue carriers). Blood carries this away along the veins, back to the heart and lungs.

Your body's central heating
Blood works like the fluid in a central heating system. It helps to spread heat evenly through your body, from busy, warm parts like the heart, to cooler areas like resting muscles.

Lung

Liver

Kidney

Heart

Lung

Spleen

Kidney

Possibly poisonous
Carbon dioxide is made by all the parts of your body. If it builds up, it becomes poisonous. Blood collects it from the tissues and takes it to the lungs, where it is breathed out.

Blood's two pumps
Your heart pushes blood around your body. Blood travels in a loop or circle, around your body and back to your heart, so your heart and blood vessels are called your *circulatory system*. In fact, the heart is really two pumps (*see page 40*).

Blood's two filters
Your kidneys are filters. Blood flows through at an amazing rate: over 500 gallons (2,000 liters) each day. Waste chemicals are filtered out of the blood, along with some water, to make urine.

Loading up with food
Digested food seeps through the lining of the small intestine into the blood. It goes to the liver, which alters some of the food so that it can be used more easily by the body. The blood then transports the food all over the body, for energy, growth, and repair.

YOUR BONES

The bones of your skeleton give your body structure and support. You have about 206 bones in your body and without them you would collapse like a heap of jelly. Each bone is a certain shape and size – which is very important for the job it must do. For example, your backbone (spine) is made up of 26 separate bones. Each one can bend and twist only a little through special joints (*see pages 60-61*) above and below it. But together, these small movements add up, so that you can bend over almost double and twist around to look to either side, upside down!

Your arm and leg bones are long and strong, like girders in a building. Where they touch other bones at their ends, they are large and rounded so that they move smoothly against each other.

Some bones, such as your shoulder-blades and hipbones, are large and flat. They are shaped like plates in order to anchor the powerful muscles that move your arms and legs. Your breastbone is also wide and flat, to anchor the muscles that raise your chest when you breathe.

The many bones in your hands and feet are moved by lots of muscles. These let you make small, delicate movements such as picking up a pin or balancing on one foot. Over half your bones are in your wrists, hands, ankles, and feet.

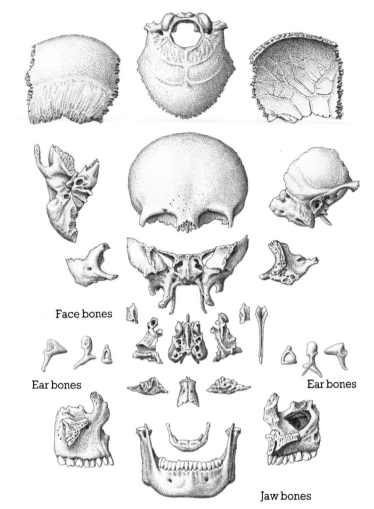

Face bones

Ear bones

Ear bones

Jaw bones

How many bones?
Count all the bones on these two pages. The human body is supposed to have about 206 bones – but where are they all?

The answer is that, as you grow, separate bones knit and fuse together solidly to form fewer, larger bones.

Inside a bone
Your bones are not hard, white, and brittle, like the dried-out bones in museums. Bones, like the thighbone shown here, are one-third water and are busy, living tissues. They need lots of blood to supply them with food. The end, or "head," of the bone is spongy inside, so as to be strong but light. The middle, or "shaft," is not solid bone for the same reason. On the outside is a living "skin" called the *periosteum*, which forms an anchorage for the various muscles and joints that attach to the bone. On the inside of some bones is the jelly-like *marrow* that makes blood cells (*see page 16*).

Spongy bone in head

Periosteum

Marrow

Dense bone in shaft

Arched for strength
Like the girders under a bridge, the top of the hip-bone is arched to give it the strength to support the body.

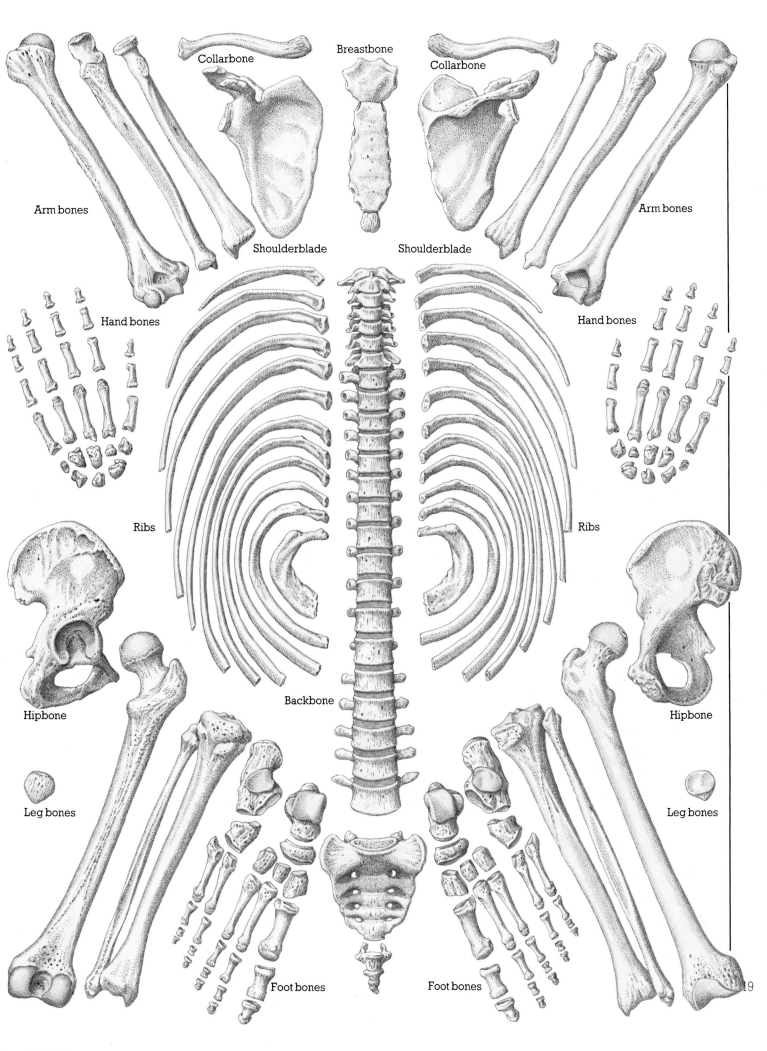

Collarbone

Breastbone

Collarbone

Arm bones

Shoulderblade

Shoulderblade

Arm bones

Hand bones

Hand bones

Ribs

Ribs

Hipbone

Hipbone

Leg bones

Backbone

Leg bones

Foot bones

Foot bones

19

THE BODY'S FRAMEWORK

Any large structure, like a building or crane or bridge, needs a framework to support it. This is usually made of girders. The architects and engineers design each girder to do a certain job. Where there is a lot of strain, thick strong girders are needed. Where stresses are small, thin girders are best because they weigh less. The bones of your body are like girders, but in many ways they are better. Bone is a living material and can change according to your body's needs. If extra stresses and strains are put on a bone, it can grow and thicken and become stronger. This sometimes happens to the bones of athletes, horseback riders, and weightlifters. If a bone breaks in an accident, the broken parts slowly join together again and the bone mends itself. (It is best if a doctor puts the broken parts back into the right positions, so that they can mend in the same shape as the original bone.) Bones also store minerals. If minerals in food are in short supply, bones release some of their minerals for use elsewhere in the body.

The skeleton skyscraper
Imagine making a huge human body. If you were to build a skyscraper, you would begin with a framework of girders. In the same way, a body needs a framework – the skeleton. This has to be a strong support for the softer parts which will be added later, and it also has to protect some of these softer parts from damage.

Protecting your nerves
In many bones, there are small holes and grooves for nerves and blood vessels. The long bones in your arm have shallow grooves in them. Nerves lie in these grooves. If the nerves lay on top of the bones, they could be damaged, because the muscles in your arm would press them against the body when they tightened.

Waving and running
The long bones in your arms and legs are thin in the middle, where there is the least stress and strain. This helps keep them as light as possible, so you can move them more easily.

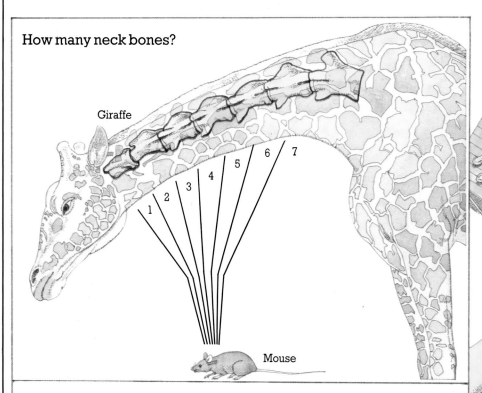

How many neck bones?

Giraffe

1 2 3 4 5 6 7

Mouse

All furry animals have roughly the same number of bones in their skeleton, but these bones are different shapes and sizes.

The animal with the longest neck, the giraffe, has seven neck bones – the same as a tiny animal like a mouse (and the same as you).

Eleven bones form three
Each of your two hipbones is made from three separate bones fused together. Together with the five bones fused to your *sacrum* (*see page 44*), they make a "ring" of eleven bones.

Spring for safety
Your ribs are thin and springy so that they absorb any knocks to your chest. If they were thick and rigid, they might crack and damage your lungs.

Muscle anchors
The bones in your lower back have thick spikes sticking out of either side. Attached to these are the powerful muscles that bend and straighten your back.

A tunnel of bone
Each of the bones in your back has a hole in it. All these holes line up to form a long tunnel down the inside of your back. Inside the tunnel is your delicate spinal cord, well protected from knocks.

Where two bones meet
Your hipbone meets your thighbone at the strong hip joint. Your hipbone is broad and flat and has a cup-shaped socket in it for the end of your thighbone.

21

THE HEAD

Thinking, seeing, hearing, smelling, tasting, eating, drinking – and taking in air. The various parts that do these vital jobs are all packed into your head. There are good reasons why the main sense organs (eyes, nose, and tongue) are near your mouth, where you take in food. Your eyes can look closely at what you eat, your nose

A hollow for the eye
This deep, rounded hole in your skull protects your eye from injury yet still lets it swivel in any direction.

A box for the brain
The upper part of your skull is the *cranium* or "brain box." It is made of eight curved bones fused together.

The far-seeing eye
Up near the top of your body, your eyes are on a "watch-tower" that gives a good view of your surroundings.

The all-knowing brain
The brain, your body's control center, receives information from your eyes, ears, nose, and mouth.

Chopping and chewing
Digestion starts here. Your teeth are fixed firmly in sockets in your jawbones. They cut off pieces of food and chew them into soft, easily swallowed lumps.

Saying yes – or no
The top two bones in your backbone are special. The upper one lets you nod your head up and down. The lower one lets you move it from side to side.

Facial control
Your face is full of nerves that connect to your brain and spinal cord. They control every movement, from eating a meal to licking your lips afterward.

Linking brain and body
Your spinal cord is like an extension of your brain into your body. In an adult, it is about 18 in (45 cm) long yet weighs just over one ounce (30 g).

can check its smell, while the taste buds on your tongue detect its flavor. This all helps to make sure that you don't eat bad food and make yourself ill. Also, your nose can smell the air you breathe, to make sure it is not stale or bad. Perched on top of your body, your head is in the best position to look around, listen and sniff for smells. Your neck is flexible so that you can look up and down and turn your head easily. If your head were near your feet you would not be able to see very far, and you'd always be breathing in dust!

Eyelid muscles
Muscles in your eyelids tighten briefly about 20,000 times each day, to wash your eyes with tear fluid.

Forehead muscles
Tensing these muscles raises your eyebrows. "Making a face" uses over 30 muscles.

Head hairs
There are about 100,000 hairs on your head. They keep in heat and protect the skin on your skull.

Eyebrow hairs
These hairs stop sweat from dripping into your eyes. They also show feelings – for example, when you frown.

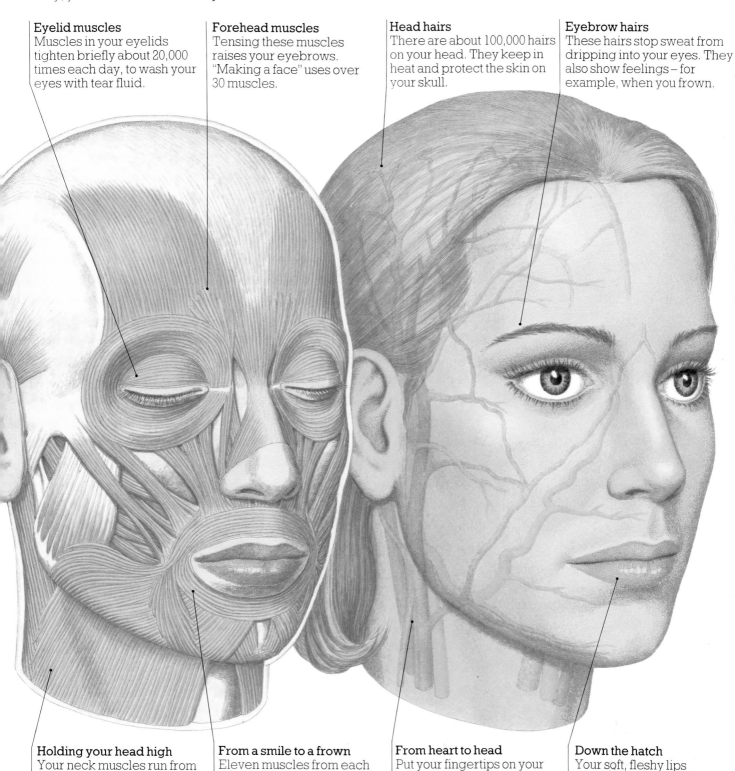

Holding your head high
Your neck muscles run from your skull to your collarbone, shoulderblades, ribs, and backbone. As you move your head, some tighten while others loosen.

From a smile to a frown
Eleven muscles from each side of your face meet at your mouth. They let your mouth and lips move and change shape when you talk, eat, smile, or frown.

From heart to head
Put your fingertips on your skin here. You can feel the blood pulsing through a large tube called the carotid artery, on its way to your brain, face, and scalp.

Down the hatch
Your soft, fleshy lips are ideal for making an airtight seal around things like straws. They are watertight too, so that liquids won't dribble out!

THE BRAIN

Many years ago, people thought that the heart controlled the body. They believed that feelings and emotions were based in the heart, since when people were frightened or worried, they felt their heart thumping. This is why we have sayings like "I know in my heart that it is true." But they were wrong. Today, we know that the heart is just a muscular pump for the blood which is controlled by the brain. In fact, the whole body is controlled by the brain.

The brain is a pink-gray, jelly-like organ weighing over 3 lb (1.5 kg). It has grooves and folds on the outside, and inside it is hollow and filled with fluid. It does not look very remarkable. Even under a powerful microscope all you can see is a tangle of nerve cells. Only recently have scientists begun to discover how these nerve cells are connected to each other and how they work together.

The brain makes up about one-fiftieth of the body's weight. Yet it uses up one-fifth of the body's energy. This amazing organ is more complicated than any computer you can think of. And that's what your brain does: think. Your brain holds your memories, feelings, and emotions. It is where you learn and know, guess and have ideas – in short, it holds your mind.

Inside the brain

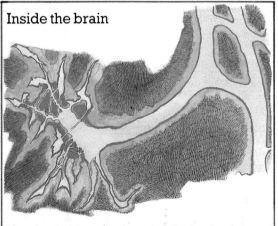

Your brain is made almost entirely of nerve cells (*see page 12*), perhaps 10,000 million of them. Each one has many thin "fingers" (*dendrites*) along which it can send signals to other nerve cells. Which route a signal takes along the dendrites depends on its particular meaning. Each nerve cell connects to thousands of others, so there is a countless number of routes a signal could take around the network.

Inside your body's headquarters
Different parts of your brain do different jobs, like the various offices at the headquarters of a large company. But the differences are not as clear-cut as in an office building. For example, memories do not seem to be stored in any one part of the brain, but all over it.

Your memory banks
No one really knows how the brain remembers. Each memory might be stored as a chemical substance or as a special nerve circuit between certain nerve cells. Some memories last only a few minutes; others can last all of your life.

Your sorting office
Your *thalamus*, deep inside your brain, acts as a kind of sorting office. It receives the messages coming in from your body and senses, then sends them on to whichever part of your brain they need to go.

Running on automatic
Your body has an "automatic pilot." It is your brain stem, the lower part of your brain near your spinal cord. It runs many parts of your body automatically. Your heart beats and your lungs breathe without your having to think about them at all.

Central control
The largest part of your brain is the cortex (*see page 26*). This is where incoming messages are sifted and decisions made about what to do. If action is needed, messages are sent out from the cortex to the right part of your body.

Messages in
Every minute your brain receives millions of nerve signals from your body. Important information must be quickly sorted out from run-of-the-mill messages. The distant sound of traffic might not be very interesting – but the smell of smoke could be vital.

Messages out
Millions of nerve signals leave the brain every minute, going to your muscles and telling them what to do. Learning a new activity, such as riding a bicycle, needs great concentration. With practice, you can do it without really thinking. The same thing happened when you learned to walk and talk.

Brain and body
Your spinal cord links your brain to your body. Your brain and spinal cord together make up your *central nervous system*. Nerves branch out from the base of your brain and from your spinal cord and go to every part of your body, carrying signals and messages back and forth. These nerves make up your *peripheral nervous system*.

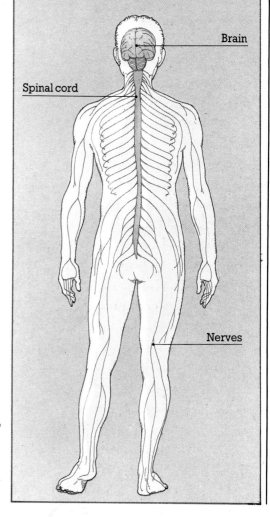

Brain

Spinal cord

Nerves

THE BRAIN MAP

The main parts of your brain are the two *cerebral cortexes*. Scientists have discovered that certain parts of the cortex deal with signals coming in from certain parts of the body. Other parts control signals going out. We can draw a "map" on the cortex showing which part, or center, of the brain is linked to part of the body. However, the centers are not in the same positions as the parts of the body. The map is all jumbled up.

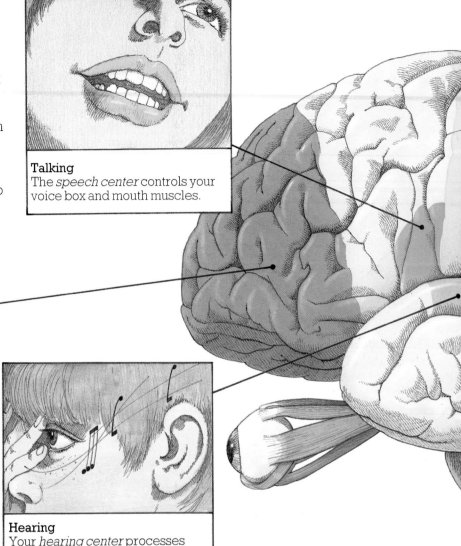

Talking
The *speech center* controls your voice box and mouth muscles.

Thinking
Thoughts are spread over the front of your cortex.

Hearing
Your *hearing center* processes messages from your ears.

Your body on your brain
This drawing of the brain "map" is from the left side. The eye is in its real position on the left, with the brain stem (which connects to the spinal cord) at the bottom.

The two sides of the brain

Did you know that the left side of your brain is linked to the right side of your body? Nerves connecting to your brain and spinal cord cross to the opposite side, so when you move your right arm, the signals telling you to move it are coming from the left side of your brain. The two halves of the brain do not work in exactly the same way. In most people, the left side of the brain is better at dealing with words and numbers, and solving problems. The right side is better at artistic and musical activities.

Mathematician Chess player Dancer

Scientist Artist Musician

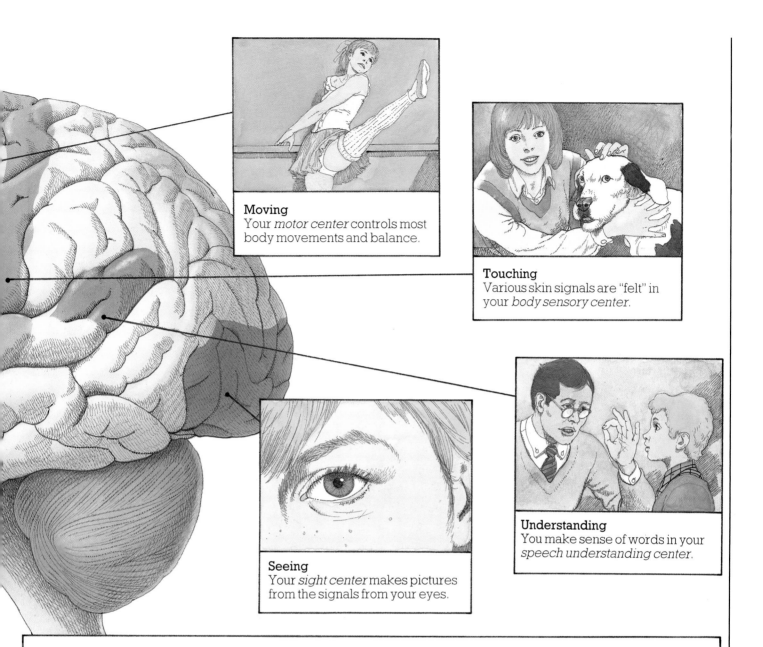

Moving
Your *motor center* controls most body movements and balance.

Touching
Various skin signals are "felt" in your *body sensory center*.

Understanding
You make sense of words in your *speech understanding center*.

Seeing
Your *sight center* makes pictures from the signals from your eyes.

Animal brains

Different animals have brains of various shapes and sizes. By studying which parts of the brain are best developed in a certain animal, and how that animal lives, we can gain an idea of what that part does.

Snake
The snake's brain has three main parts, each about the same size. The back part controls basic processes such as heartbeat.

Bird
A bird does not think, but the middle part of its brain is highly developed. This part controls the bird's wide range of movements.

Mammal
In a cat the front parts of the brain are much bigger. These are involved in thinking behavior – what we call "intelligence."

Human
In human brains the front parts are so big that they cover almost all other parts. This explains our great intelligence.

THE FIVE SENSES

How do you find out about the world around you? You look, listen, smell, taste, and touch. Doing so, you are using five senses and your eyes, ears, nose, tongue, and skin are your main sense organs. Over the next eight pages, you can see how these senses work and how important they are to you.

In fact, you have more than five senses. The sense of touch is really several different senses. You can feel light touch, heavy pressure, heat and cold, movements and vibrations, and pain.

There is a different sense of "feeling," inside your muscles, which tells you how relaxed or contracted they are. Using this sense (the "position sense") you can tell what positions your body, arms, and legs are in without looking. You can close your eyes and touch each fingertip in turn.

Another of your senses helps you to stand upright and not fall down – your sense of balance. This is a combination of what the balance organs in your ears tell you (*see page 33*), what your eyes see, and what your skin and muscles (especially the soles of your feet) feel.

A sensitive person
Your skin does not have the same degree of sensitivity all over. When you want to feel something very carefully you use your fingertips, because these are very sensitive. The skin there has more nerve endings than anywhere else (see page 12). In the person on the right, the most sensitive parts of the skin are drawn biggest. You can see that your fingers, toes, and lips are very sensitive. This is why babies put things into their mouths to find out what shape they are and what they feel like.

Keeping in touch

Your skin tells you about more than just the shape and texture of the things you touch. There are many different kinds of nerve endings just under the surface of your skin, which tell you different things about the outside world.

You can feel heat or cold. For instance, you can tell whether the air around you is warm or cool. When water splashes on you, you feel a combination of touch and cold. Sometimes you feel only light touch, as when you walk on a sandy beach and the grains of sand press evenly all over the soles of your feet. But when you come to sharp pebbles, the edges of the pebbles press hard on your feet. This can be uncomfortable. If any pressure becomes too heavy it begins to hurt, because it sets off special nerve endings in your skin. The pain tells you that your body is in danger of being damaged.

How animals sense the world
Different animals sense their surroundings in different ways. Each part of this dog and cat is drawn according to how sensitive it is. The dog's large nose shows it has a very good sense of smell, and its whiskers can feel well. Its big tongue means it has a keen sense of taste. A dog's eyes are not that good, especially compared to the cat, whose enormous eyes show that it has very sharp sight. The cat's huge ears mean it can hear well too. All this is for a reason. Cats hunt at night, so they need good eyes and ears in the dark. Dogs hunt mainly by sniffing around for scent.

Dog

Cat

THE EYE

Of all our senses, our sight is the most important. A scientist worked out that four-fifths of everything you remember is something you have seen, from the beauty of the setting sun, to learning multiplication at school.

Even more amazing is that your picture of the world is only slightly larger than a postage stamp. This is the area inside your eye where the picture is detected by nerve cells. These nerve cells are spread out in the *retina*, which lines the inside of the eye. There are two special types of cells, called *rods* and *cones*.

There are over 100 million rods in each eye. They see in black and white (not color) and work well in poor light. There are about seven million cones in each eye. The cones see colors and fine details, but work only in bright light. Each time light hits a rod or cone it generates a nerve signal, which travels out of your eye and along the main nerve to your brain. At the brain's sight center (*see page 27*) all these impulses are put together. The black-and-white and color pictures are combined, as are the pictures from your two eyes. The eye simply turns light rays into nerve impulses and sends them on. It is in your brain that you actually "see."

Seeing in "wide-screen"
Like a giant movie screen, the front part of your eye projects a picture of what is outside on to the back part. The picture moves all the time. Even when you stare steadily, your eyes still dart around.

A clear view
The curved part at the front of the eye is the *cornea*. It is crystal clear, and its shape bends light rays as they pass through, helping the lens to focus them. The very thin layer on the surface of the cornea is the *conjunctiva*. This is also clear and it is very sensitive, feeling when the smallest bit of dust lands on it.

A sharp picture
Like a camera, the eye has to focus so that the picture you see is clear and sharp. The *lens* at the front of the eye does the focusing. Muscles around it tighten and pull it thinner or relax to let it get thicker. A thin lens focuses faraway objects, while a thick lens focuses near ones.

Just enough light
The colored part of your eye is called the *iris*. It controls the amount of light entering your eye by making the hole in its center larger or smaller. In dim light the hole is large. In bright light it gets very small, to protect the sensitive nerve cells at the back of your eye.

Lens

Why two eyes?	Blinking	Crying
Each eye sees a different view of an object – close one eye, then the other, to see the difference. Also, the eyes swivel in to look at nearby things but look straight ahead at distant things. The brain uses this information to judge distance.	For about half an hour each day you cannot see – you are blinking. Your eyelids sweep across the delicate eye surface and spread a fresh film of tear fluid. This washes away dust and germs. A blink lasts about one-third of a second.	No one knows why we cry. Your eyes "water" when dirt gets in them, to wash them clean. Tear fluid goes down tiny holes in the inner parts of the eyelid, into the nose. This is why you blow your nose when you have been crying.

Outer covering
(*conjunctiva*)

Tough outer case
(*sclera*)

Blood-rich layer
(*choroid*)

Picking up the picture

The *retina* at the back of your eye detects the light rays and turns them into nerve signals. This is where the rods and cones are. Because of the way the lens works, the picture on the retina is always upside down. But your brain automatically turns it right-side up.

Optive nerve to brain

A ball of jelly

Inside the eye is a clear jelly-like fluid. This keeps the eye ball-shaped so that it can swivel smoothly in its socket as you look around. The whole eye is contained in a tough outer coat called the *sclera*. Just inside this is a blood-rich nourishing layer, called the *choroid*.

Animal eyes

Different animals see the world in various ways. Humans have better vision than many other animals.

Maybe our ancestors hunted and found ripe fruits and other foods by sight, rather than by smell.

Seeing in the dark

An owl hunts at night. Its eyes are huge, to collect what little light there is. They also face forward, to judge distance accurately.

Keeping an all-around watch

A mouse is active mainly at dawn and dusk, so it has large eyes. They stick out from its head so that it can watch for danger all around.

Hundreds of eyes

An insect has two "eyes," each made of hundreds of tiny flat parts. It probably sees the world like a mosaic, in overlapping segments.

THE EAR

Imagine dozing in a field in the summer sun. Suddenly a jet plane roars overhead. As the noise fades away, you can hear the quiet humming of bees and the birds singing in the distance. The jet makes a noise a billion times louder than the bees and birds – but your ears can hear them both. You can also hear sounds ranging from the low notes of a double bass to the high sound of a cymbal.

The part of the ear you can see is called the outer ear. This simply collects sound waves and funnels them into your ear canal. The important parts of your ear are buried 1½ in (3.8 cm) inside your head, just behind and below your eye. These inner parts are well protected, surrounded by your skull. They turn sound waves into electrical nerve signals and send them to your brain. In your brain the signals are sorted out and you "hear."

Having two ears is very useful. If a sound comes from one side, the sound waves reach one ear a split second before they get to the other. Your brain detects this time difference and can tell you where the sound is coming from.

Music to your ears

Your ear is an amazing and delicate organ. It can hear all the complicated sound waves made by an orchestra. It can detect loudness (volume) and high and low notes (pitch). From the signals it sends to your brain, you can pick out the sound of each instrument even when they are all being played at once.

Your ear trumpet

Your outer ear is made of the ear flap, on the outside, and your ear canal, a tube leading inward. Many animals move their ears to detect where a sound comes from. People cannot, although some can wiggle their ears.

A sticky problem

The skin on the inside of your ear canal makes a sticky substance called earwax. Floating dust and dirt stick to it, keeping your inner ear clean. As you chew and talk, your face muscles move the lining of the canal and old wax slowly works its way out.

Banging the drum

When you bang a drum, it shakes or *vibrates* and makes the air around it move, forming sound waves. Your eardrum works in the opposite way. Sound waves hit it and make it vibrate. The vibrations pass along three tiny bones called the hammer, anvil, and stirrup. (Notice their shapes.)

The ear machine

Sounds go through many different forms before they reach your brain. They start out as sound waves in the air, then reach your eardrum and three tiny bones. Vibrations pass through the fluid inside your inner ear, in the cochlea. Finally they are converted to electrical signals and sent along nerves to your brain. A homemade model of the ear might look something like this.

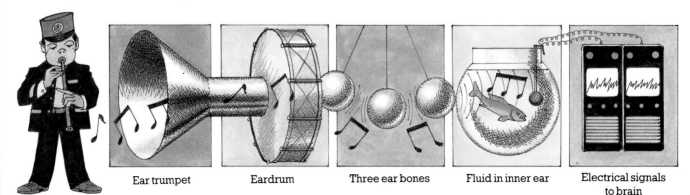

Ear trumpet Eardrum Three ear bones Fluid in inner ear Electrical signals to brain

Semicircular canals

Three ear bones

The curly tube that hears

The inner part of your ear is extremely complicated. The large snail-shaped tube is called the *cochlea*. It contains nerve cells which have tiny hairs sticking into a fluid. Vibrations passed on by the three tiny bones move the fluid, which moves the hairs, making nerve signals. There are over 20,000 nerve cells in each ear, and up to 100 hairs on each cell. Different parts of the cochlea can detect high and low notes.

Nerves to brain

Keeping your balance

Your ears not only hear, but also help to keep your balance. The semicircular canals in the big picture (*left*) contain fluid. As your head tilts, the fluid swirls about and tiny hair cells (like the ones in the cochlea) detect its movements. There are also tiny clumps of crystal on the hairs. As you change position, gravity pulls the crystals down and bends the hairs. This sends signals to your brain, telling it how you are positioned.

From ear to throat

A narrow tube, the *Eustachian tube*, runs from inside your ear to the back of your throat. When you swallow, chew, or yawn, the entrance to the tube opens and air can travel in or out of your middle ear. This makes the air pressure on both sides of your eardrum the same, which means that your eardrum can vibrate easily and you can hear properly.

INSIDE YOUR MOUTH

Your mouth is the first stop for the food you eat. Each part of it does a certain job. Your teeth chop, chew, and crush large pieces of food into small ones. Your tongue moves pieces of food around so that your teeth can get at them, and it pushes the pieces to the top of your throat to swallow them. Your salivary glands make a watery liquid that moistens food so that it slips easily down to your stomach. And your whole mouth warms up cold food and cools down hot food. Everything you put into your mouth is changed into small, soggy lumps that you can swallow. All this helps you to digest your food more easily later on. Your mouth also shapes the sounds from your voice box (in your throat) into words. Try making the same noise and moving your lips, tongue, teeth, and cheeks to see how many different sounds you can make.

The food processors

Inside your mouth it is dark, moist, and warm. These are good conditions for germs which feed on old bits of food. Although the germs don't make you very ill, they can harm your teeth. This is why you should clean your teeth after meals.

Grooves in the gum

Your gums help to hold your teeth securely in their sockets. There is a groove around each tooth, where the gum is joined to it. This is a favorite place for germs to lurk.

Choppers

Your four front teeth at the top and bottom are called incisors. They are sharp and chop off bits of food when you bite. Next to them are canines, which are more pointed but still good choppers.

Crushers

The rest of your teeth, toward the back of your mouth, are broad and flat. They crush and chew food. The three big teeth on each side at the very back are molars. The two in front are premolars.

Inside a tooth

Here is one of your crushing teeth, a molar, cut away to show what is inside. The top part of the tooth, above the gum, is the crown. The lower parts, the roots, anchor the tooth firmly in your jawbone. The tooth's outer layer is enamel, the hardest substance in your body. This is just as well since it has to crunch through nuts and other tough foods. Inside is a layer of dentine, which is quite hard but can absorb bumps and knocks. Enamel and dentine have no blood vessels or nerves, so they cannot feel anything. Inside the dentine is the pulp. This has many blood vessels and nerves. If you have a toothache, it is because something has gone through both the enamel and the dentine and is affecting the nerves in the pulp.

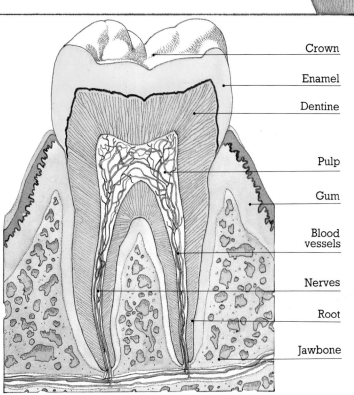

Crown

Enamel

Dentine

Pulp

Gum

Blood vessels

Nerves

Root

Jawbone

Mouth-watering

Saliva is a watery liquid made by glands under your jaws, in front of your ears, and under your tongue. It helps you to digest and swallow your food. It also helps to keep your mouth and teeth clean.

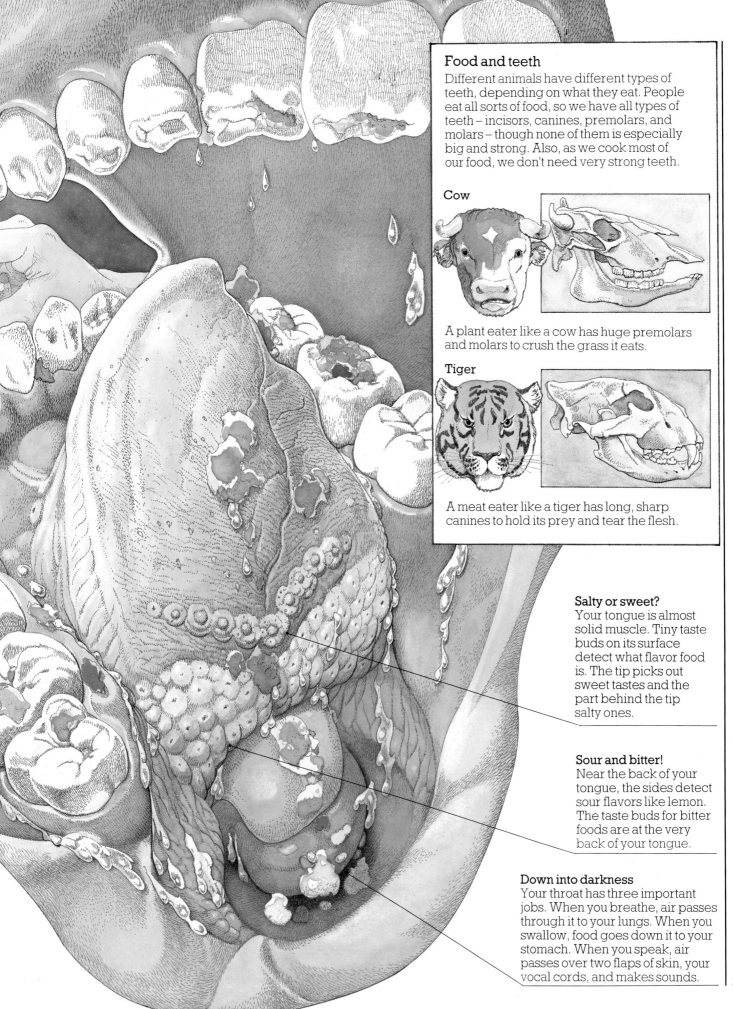

Food and teeth

Different animals have different types of teeth, depending on what they eat. People eat all sorts of food, so we have all types of teeth – incisors, canines, premolars, and molars – though none of them is especially big and strong. Also, as we cook most of our food, we don't need very strong teeth.

Cow

A plant eater like a cow has huge premolars and molars to crush the grass it eats.

Tiger

A meat eater like a tiger has long, sharp canines to hold its prey and tear the flesh.

Salty or sweet?

Your tongue is almost solid muscle. Tiny taste buds on its surface detect what flavor food is. The tip picks out sweet tastes and the part behind the tip salty ones.

Sour and bitter!

Near the back of your tongue, the sides detect sour flavors like lemon. The taste buds for bitter foods are at the very back of your tongue.

Down into darkness

Your throat has three important jobs. When you breathe, air passes through it to your lungs. When you swallow, food goes down it to your stomach. When you speak, air passes over two flaps of skin, your vocal cords, and makes sounds.

THE CHEST

Your chest is the powerhouse of your body. Every few seconds, every hour of every day, your chest muscles contract to make your lungs breathe in air. The oxygen in the air passes through your lungs into your blood. Your heart then pumps this blood all around your body – every second, every hour of every day. All the parts of your

Bone and blade
Your collarbone at the front and shoulderblade at the back anchor the many muscles that move your arm. You can swing your arm around in a circle.

A rod at the back
The part of the backbone at the back of your chest is quite stiff compared to the rest of the backbone. This helps to hold your lungs properly for easy breathing.

Well-oiled breathing
Your lungs are covered by two thin, smooth layers of tissue with a slippery fluid like oil between them. This helps to make breathing movements easier.

A place for your heart
Your heart is slightly to the left side of your body. Your left lung is a little smaller than your right lung, as it has a slight hollow in it where your heart sits.

A cage at the front
Your ribs make a strong cage that protects your lungs and heart. But they are also hinged, so that they can move up and down as you breathe.

Spare ribs
Most people have 12 pairs of ribs, but some have 11 or 13 pairs. Each pair joins to a vertebra in the backbone. The top 7 pairs join to your breastbone.

Record-breaking liver
Your liver is your busiest organ. It deals with at least 500 different body chemicals and produces much of the heat that keeps your body warm.

Second stop for food
Your stomach carries on the job started by your mouth. It breaks down your food and churns it up with powerful chemicals, often for three hours or more.

body need a constant supply of fresh blood, carrying plentiful oxygen. Without it, life would soon stop. Because your lungs and heart are right next to each other, blood has hardly any distance to go after it is replenished with oxygen, before it is pumped to the rest of your body. This means your body receives the freshest blood possible.

Some of your digestive organs, such as your liver and stomach, are within your rib cage. They lie under a dome-shaped sheet of muscle called your *diaphragm* which you use to breathe.

Muscles under muscles
There are several layers of muscles around your chest. They each do slightly different jobs. This one helps to pull your shoulder down and forward.

Muscles over muscles
This large sheet-like muscle is just under your skin. It is very strong. It pulls your arm forward and helps to lift your body when you are hanging from a bar.

Making milk
In women, the breasts are large glands that make milk to feed a newborn baby. Men also have these glands but they are very small and do not make milk.

Blood for brain
Deep in your chest, arteries divide and run upward to supply blood to your arms, head, and brain. Another artery goes down behind your heart.

A dome that pulls down
The dome-shaped sheet of muscle under your chest is your diaphragm. When it contracts, it pulls your lungs down, making them bigger, and you breathe in.

Holes in the dome
The diaphragm has gaps for important tubes, such as the esophagus taking food to your stomach and blood vessels running to and from your heart.

Padded for protection
A layer of fat and skin cover the chest to protect it. As in other parts of the body, women usually have slightly more fatty tissue under their skin than men.

Blood for your lower half
Two large blood vessels run between your chest and abdomen. The main artery carries fresh blood down while the main vein brings stale blood back.

THE LUNGS

How long can you hold your breath? A minute, or even two? Much longer and your body tells you to start breathing again, because breathing brings fresh air into it and this contains oxygen, which is vital for you to keep living.

Your lungs are expertly designed to absorb as much oxygen as possible from the air. They also get rid of the waste substance carbon dioxide. When you breathe in, air contains nearly 21 percent oxygen. On the way out, this is down to 16 percent; the extra 4 or 5 percent is made up of carbon dioxide. Your breathing is controlled by your brain. When your muscles work harder they need more oxygen, which they take from your blood, and so the oxygen level of blood falls (and its carbon dioxide level rises). Your brain detects this and orders your breathing muscles to work harder and faster, to bring in more oxygen. When full, your lungs hold three quarts (about three liters) of air. While you are resting or asleep, you take about one breath every three or four seconds. At the end of a footrace you could be "gasping for breath" twice a second, and taking in 15 times as much air as usual.

Inside the lungs

The bigger the surface for absorbing oxygen, the more oxygen you can absorb. In each lung there are over 300 million tiny "air bubbles" called *alveoli*. If you spread the bubble walls out flat, they would cover a tennis court! Hairs in the nose and the sticky linings of the air passages filter the air you breathe in, to clean it before it enters the lungs.

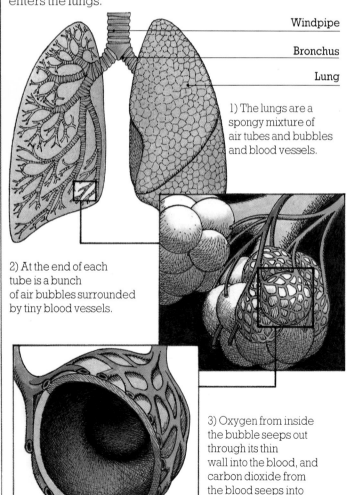

Windpipe

Bronchus

Lung

1) The lungs are a spongy mixture of air tubes and bubbles and blood vessels.

2) At the end of each tube is a bunch of air bubbles surrounded by tiny blood vessels.

3) Oxygen from inside the bubble seeps out through its thin wall into the blood, and carbon dioxide from the blood seeps into the bubble.

As you breathe in

The sheet of muscle at the base of your chest is your *diaphragm*. When slack and relaxed, it forms a dome shape, and your lungs are small (as shown). To breathe in, it contracts and flattens. The muscles between your ribs also contract to pull the ribs up and out. These actions make your chest bigger and stretch the lungs inside. Air is sucked in through your mouth and down your windpipe.

The ins and outs of breathing

Your lungs (and your heart) fill your chest. Air tubes called bronchi run up from them to the main air tube, your windpipe (trachea), which connects to your throat. Breathing in uses two main sets of muscles between the ribs and the bottom of the chest. Breathing out happens automatically when you relax these muscles.

As you breathe out
When your lungs are at their biggest (as in the picture), you relax the diaphragm and rib muscles. The lungs spring back from their stretched size to their smaller size. Air is pushed out of them and up your windpipe. This air contains water vapor, which condenses on a cold day and makes your breath "steamy."

Sneezing

You close your throat while air pressure builds up in your lungs. When you suddenly let the air out, it blows dust and germs from your nose.

Hiccuping

A hiccup is made when your diaphragm contracts more violently than it usually does. It can be caused by eating or drinking too quickly.

Yawning

You yawn when bored or tired. It may be that you are not breathing deeply enough and carbon dioxide has built up. A yawn might clear it out.

Laughing

Laughter is sudden jerks of the diaphragm which force air up the windpipe and through the voice box. Trying to stop can make it worse!

THE HEART

Blood is the body's transportation system. At the center of this system is your heart. It has four chambers with muscular walls. About once a second, the walls contract and squeeze blood out of the chambers into strong tubes, called arteries. The blood is pushed around your body. As the heart relaxes again, its chambers fill with more blood brought back to it by other tubes, the veins. This pumping, called a heartbeat, happens every second of every day, for as long as you live. You can feel blood surging through the artery in your wrist. Each surge or "pulse" is one heartbeat. Your "pulse rate" tells you how fast your heart is beating.

No man-made pump is as reliable as your heart. It can beat for 100 years or more without a rest. It can also beat faster or slower and change how much blood it pumps into each beat, depending on how active you are. The adjustments are controlled by nerves from your brain and by hormones. When you are resting your heart might beat 60 to 70 times a minute, and pump one-eighth of a pint (about 70 ml) of blood each time. When you run a race, your heart beats over twice as fast and pumps three times as much blood with each beat.

The traffic junction

The heart is like a traffic junction. Arteries and veins lead in and out of it, taking blood to where it is needed. In fact, the heart is not one pump but two, side by side. The right side sends stale blood which has been around your body (the blue carriers in the picture) to the lungs. There it collects oxygen (the red carriers), and then flows back to the left side of the heart, which pumps it all around your body. When it returns it has given up its oxygen (blue carriers again) and flows back to the heart's right side.

To right lung

From right lung

Back from the body

Stale blood flows from your body back to your heart along thin-walled, floppy tubes called veins. By the time blood has passed through all your tissues it no longer moves in powerful surges, as it does in the arteries, so the veins do not need strong walls. Some veins have one-way valves, to make sure blood keeps flowing in the right direction.

From body and legs

How the heart pumps

Each side of the heart has two chambers. The upper one (*atrium*) is small and has thin walls. It swells as blood flows into it. The blood then passes through a valve to the lower chamber (*ventricle*). This is bigger and has a thick, muscular wall. The left lower chamber pushes blood all around your body, from your head to your toes. The right lower chamber is slightly smaller and sends blood to your lungs. (The labels here may seem the wrong way around because it's your right side, facing you.)

| Blood from body | Blood from lungs | Upper chambers contract | Blood flows into lower chambers | Blood flows out of lower chambers | Blood from body | Blood to body | Blood to lungs | Blood from lungs |

1 — Upper chambers relax

2 — Lower chambers relax

3 — Lower chambers contract

4 — Cycle is complete

Loading with oxygen
Your pulmonary arteries carry blood from your heart to your lungs. Unlike other arteries, they contain stale blood with no oxygen in it. In your lungs, the blood gets rid of waste and carbon dioxide (blue loads) and picks up oxygen (red loads).

From head and arms

To head and right arm

To head

To left arm

Delivering the goods
Fresh with oxygen, blood is pumped out through your main arteries to your body. The arteries have strong, elastic walls to cope with the powerful surge of blood when the heart beats. The arteries branch out and each one takes blood to a different part of your body.

To left lung

Power of the pump
The heart is such a powerful pump that it takes about one minute on average for each blood cell to travel around your body. In one day the heart could pump enough liquid to fill a 2,500-gallon (10,000-liter) tanker.

1 hour

8 hours

16 hours

24 hours

To body and legs

From left lung

One-way road ahead
Valves in your heart make sure that the blood flows the right way. There is a valve between each upper and lower chamber, and another one where blood leaves your heart to flow into the main artery. As the valves snap shut they make the "lub dub" sound of a heartbeat.

41

ARMS AND HANDS

Look closely at your arms and hands. They are so well designed that they can do an enormous variety of jobs, from threading a needle to lifting a sack of potatoes. Besides moving and handling, they can feel. The skin on your fingertips is very sensitive and can detect movements too small to see.

It is difficult for engineers to copy the design of the arm and hand for use in a machine. The computer-controlled "robot arms" in car factories are similar to our arms in some ways, but they are much simpler. They can do only a few simple tasks and they soon wear out. The human arm lasts for years and years. It can mend itself when injured, and it is controlled by the most complicated computer of all: the human brain.

Why does the human body have hands and arms? Why aren't we four-legged, like dogs and cats and so many other animals? The reason probably has to do with feeding. Our monkey-like ancestors lived among the trees, using all four limbs to move about. But they also used their front limbs to pick fruits, shoots, leaves and flowers, to catch small animals, and to put these things into their mouths to eat. When the first humans began to walk on two legs, their arms were not needed to help them move about anymore. Gradually these early people learned that they could pick up and fiddle with other things besides food. Pieces of stone, wood, and bone could be made into tools and used to carry out tasks. The human body has a clever brain, but it is the arms, hands, and fingers that make it possible to carry out many of its ideas.

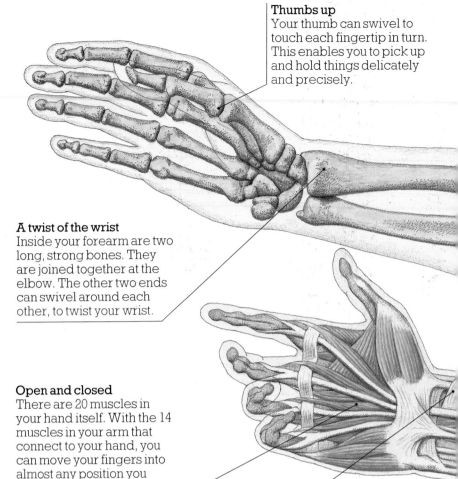

Thumbs up
Your thumb can swivel to touch each fingertip in turn. This enables you to pick up and hold things delicately and precisely.

A twist of the wrist
Inside your forearm are two long, strong bones. They are joined together at the elbow. The other two ends can swivel around each other, to twist your wrist.

Open and closed
There are 20 muscles in your hand itself. With the 14 muscles in your arm that connect to your hand, you can move your fingers into almost any position you wish.

Two levers for your hand
Under its skin, your arm is made mostly of muscles and bones. Your upper arm and forearm work like two adjustable levers, so that you can put your hand exactly where you want it. Your palm and fingers do the grasping, gripping and – just as important – letting go.

Wrist bands
Just about where you wear a watch, there are ligaments – bands of tough, stringy tissue wrapped around your wrist to strengthen it. Under them slide long, thin *tendons* that work your fingers. There are over 20 tendons in each wrist.

Inside a fingertip
Imagine walking about with your eyes closed. You would probably hold your hands out in front of you so that your fingers could feel for anything in the way. The skin of your fingertips is packed with nerve endings that can detect the lightest touch (*see page 12*) as well as heat, cold and pain. The hard nail at the back of your fingertip gives the skin something solid to be squeezed against as you feel things. Without a nail, your fingertip would bend when you touched something and you would not be able to feel so well.

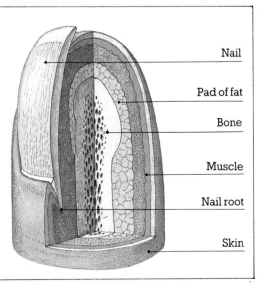

Nail

Pad of fat

Bone

Muscle

Nail root

Skin

Animal "nails"
Your nails are made of a tough substance that is like hardened skin. The claws, hooves, and horns of other animals are made of the same substance, which is called *keratin*. Because we do not use our "claws" for tearing up food or fighting (not usually, anyway), they have become much smaller than the claws of many animals. Your nails grow about one millimeter in two weeks, and your fingernails grow slightly faster than your toenails. Both your fingernails and toenails grow more slowly in the winter.

42

A groove to move in
Your upper-arm bone has two grooves in it at the lower end. The ends of your two forearm bones move smoothly along these grooves as you bend your elbow.

Feeling your pulse
An artery passes between your skin and your wrist bones. Press on it and you can feel blood pumping through with each heartbeat. This is your pulse.

Getting a grip
Clench your fist and you will see some of the muscles that move your fingers are in your forearm. You can see them rippling under the skin.

Useful veins
Inside your forearm, just under the skin, are veins carrying blood back to your heart. Doctors usually take blood samples from these veins.

Bulging muscles
Bend your elbow and tense the muscles in your upper arm. As they shorten they become fatter, bulging under your skin.

The hawk's talons

A hawk uses its strong, sharp talons for seizing hold of its prey as it swoops, and for holding the prey while it tears it apart with its sharp beak.

The bear's claws

Bears eat most kinds of food. They hunt for fish and small animals, and dig for roots. Their claws are not particularly sharp, but they are strong.

The horse's hooves

Most animals have five "claws" on each leg. A horse has only one – the hoof. This has become large and strong to support the horse's weight.

The goat's horns

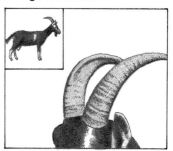

Some animals have horns which are made from hardened skin with bone inside. The goat uses its horns to defend itself when it is frightened.

THE ABDOMEN

The lower half of the main body is called your abdomen. Inside it, many organs are squashed together. They have to do mainly with the "ins" and "outs" of food – taking new food into the body, and getting rid of the old food and other unwanted things. Most of the space is taken up by your intestines, the "in" organs. They digest food

The base of your back
The wedge-shaped bone at the bottom of your back is called the *sacrum*. It is made of five separate bones that merge into one bone while you are a child.

Keep a straight back
Five strong bones in the back of your abdomen carry the weight of your head, arms, and body. If you bend badly here, you can get a backache.

Long and thin
Packed into your abdomen, and filling most of its lower part, are the coils of your small intestine. Here digested food is absorbed into your bloodstream.

Shorter and wider
Your large intestine is shorter than your small intestine, but much wider. It curls around your small intestine and absorbs spare water from leftover food.

A bowl of bone
Your hipbone, made of several bones joined together, is shaped like a bowl. It helps to protect the soft organs in the lower part of your abdomen.

A strange "tail"
At the very base of your backbone is your "tail" or *coccyx*. It is made of three or four small bones joined into one. In some animals, the bones are much longer.

A new life
In a woman the base of the abdomen contains the ovaries (which hold the eggs) and the womb, where a baby grows. In a man, this place contains intestines.

Waste disposal
Your bladder stores urine from your kidneys. Behind it (in women) is the womb. As your bladder slowly fills with urine, it puts pressure on your intestines.

and absorb it into your bloodstream, so that it can be carried around your body. They let any food that cannot be digested pass straight through. Your liver and kidneys are the main "out" organs. They filter blood and deal with the unwanted things it brings from other parts of the body. This keeps your blood clear of waste matter, which would build up and become poisonous if it were not removed. The organs in your abdomen rarely stay still. Your intestines, especially, squirm and squeeze as they push food along.

Four sets of muscles
There are four sets of muscles that strengthen the front of your abdomen. Three of them are flat sheets; this one runs diagonally.

Muscles on your side
This layer of muscle is the innermost of the three sheets. It runs from your front around to your back, in part of your chest as well as your abdomen.

An uphill struggle
Next to the artery is the main vein taking blood from your abdomen and legs to your heart. As you walk, your leg muscles push blood up this vein.

Where the lifeline was
In the womb the umbilical cord was your "lifeline." After birth (*see pages 54-55*) it was cut and the end dropped off, leaving your navel.

A strong strap
Inside the three sheets of muscle is this strap-shaped muscle. It runs from the front of your hipbone to your ribs. One such muscle is on each side of your abdomen.

Crisscrossed for strength
The outermost of the three sheets of muscle runs diagonally. With the up-and-down and side-to-side sets of muscles, the front of the abdomen is very strong.

Fight the flab
In some people the skin over the abdomen is full of fat. The fat is a food store for times of need. Too much fat is unhealthy and means that you eat too much.

Blood for the abdomen
The main artery from your heart runs down just inside your backbone. Branches of it fork off to your intestines, liver, kidneys, and other abdominal organs.

WHERE YOUR FOOD GOES

You swallow some food, and for you it seems like the end of the matter. But for your food it is only the beginning. Ahead lies an amazing journey lasting perhaps two days, traveling through more than 25 ft (8 m) of tubes, chambers, and pipes. These make up your digestive system. The job of the digestive system is to take what you eat and break it down (*digest it*) into pieces tiny enough to be absorbed into your body.

The digestive system is one long tube, starting at the mouth and ending at the anus. But some parts of the tube are narrow, others are wide. Some parts of it are long and others are short. The shape of each part depends on what it does.

Swallowed food takes several seconds to go down your throat and then down a muscular tube which is called your food pipe, or *esophagus*. It ends up in your stomach. Here it is crushed and squashed and mixed with digestive chemicals into a thick, creamy soup. From your stomach, the liquid food is squeezed slowly into your small intestine. Here, the useful bits of food pass through the lining of the tube and into your bloodstream.

Meanwhile, the leftover bits of food pass into a shorter, wider tube, your large intestine. Here, most of the water is absorbed from the leftovers and they become more solid. Finally they are stored at the end of your large intestine, until it's convenient to get rid of them.

Only some parts of food are taken into your body. These useful bits are called *nutrients*. They will be used for body-building, growth and repair, and to give you energy. The leftover parts of food are not digested, but this does not mean they are useless. Some indigestible parts help your digestive system to grip the food as it passes slowly through the tubes. This useful but undigested food is called *fiber*.

When you swallow food it seems to go "into" your body. But this is not really true. The food goes into the tunnel that runs through your digestive system, like the hole in a pipe. But it cannot get into your organs and tissues until it is absorbed through the lining of the small intestine. Only then is the food truly inside your body.

The destruction line

In many factories, goods are put together piece by piece on a "production line." Your digestive system does the opposite. It pulls your food apart, bit by bit. So it is not a production line, it's a "destruction line." On the next four pages you can see a slightly untangled view of the stomach and other digestive organs, with a day's worth of meals passing through at various stages.

Pushing food along
Food doesn't just fall down into your stomach. The muscles in your esophagus wall contract to make a sort of "traveling wave" that pushes the food in front of it. This is called *peristalsis*. It means you can swallow even when you are lying down! In fact, food is pushed through your entire digestive system by peristalsis.

Dealing with nutrients
Your liver receives blood full of freshly digested nutrients from your small intestine. The liver sorts out the nutrients. It stores some, changes some, and lets others pass through to other parts of the body.

Esophagus

Liver

Four-in-one stomach
A cow's stomach has not just one chamber, like yours, but four chambers. Chewed grass goes first into the rumen, where it is partly digested. Later, the cow brings up this food and chews it some more ("chewing the cud"). Then it is swallowed again and goes into the other chambers. This double digestion helps the cow to get maximum nourishment from tough grasses and plants.

Rumen

Reticulum

Omasum

Abomasum

A bag for your lunch

Your packed lunch is in a box all morning and a bag all afternoon – your stomach. Muscles in the stomach wall crush the food to a pulp. Its lining makes acids and other chemicals that dissolve the food.

Chemical attack

Digestive juices are made in your pancreas, which is just under your stomach. They flow along a narrow tube into your duodenum, where they attack the food chemically and dissolve it into tiny pieces.

What your body needs

Most foods are alright for you to eat – as long as you don't eat too much of any one thing. Your body needs regular supplies of a good variety of food to stay healthy and keep working properly, as different types of food do different jobs. It needs protein for building new tissues, and carbohydrates and some fats for energy and bodybuilding. Vitamins help to prevent certain diseases, and fiber keeps your digestive system working well. And water, in both food and drink, is vital. You could stay alive longer without food than you could without water.

Eggs, meat, milk, cheese, and fish contain protein; butter and oils, fat; and sugar and bread, carbohydrates.

Vitamins are found mainly in fresh fruit and vegetables.

Vegetables, fruit, whole-grain bread, nuts, and beans contain fiber.

There is a lot of water in most fruits and vegetables.

Gall bladder

Dealing with fats

Fatty food is difficult to digest. The gall bladder stores bile, a digestive juice made by the liver. After a meal, bile flows down the bile duct into the duodenum. Here it begins to *emulsify* fats – break them down into tiny droplets, which the other digestive juices can then attack more easily.

Pancreas

Stomach

Small intestine

Large intestine

The beginning of the end

The first 10 in (25 cm) or so of your small intestine is called the *duodenum*. Juices flow into it from your pancreas and gall bladder. It is the beginning of the end for the food you have eaten, which will soon be absorbed by the rest of your small intestine.

Pipes, tanks, and chemicals

Like the pipes and tanks of a sewage plant, your digestive system is a series of tubes and chambers. Just as different chemicals are added to sewage at each stage, digestive juices are added to your food at different stages of its journey, to break it down. In both processes, waste is left over at the end.

1

2

3

The small intestine

This long tube snakes around your abdomen for 20 ft (6 m) or so. It continually squeezes food along inside it, by peristalsis (*see page 46*).

Absorbing nutrients

In the lining of the small intestine there are many small blood vessels. Nutrients seep into the blood and are carried away, mainly to the liver.

Small intestine

Large intestine

The large intestine
The large intestine is about 5 ft (1.5 m) long, shorter than the small intestine. But it is over twice as wide, at 2½ in (7 cm).

Absorbing water
The watery leftovers in the large intestine become more solid as water is absorbed from them. Useful bacteria live here, making important vitamins.

Inside the liver and kidneys
Your liver is in several parts, or *lobes*. It has a very rich blood flow. As well as dealing with the nutrients from digestion, it stores the energy-giving substances glucose and starch. It also stores vitamins and breaks down old blood cells.

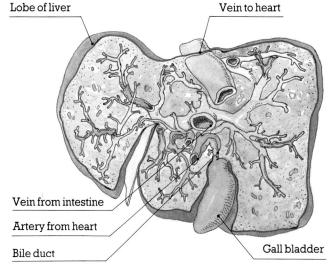

Lobe of liver

Vein to heart

Vein from intestine

Artery from heart

Bile duct

Gall bladder

Your kidneys are blood filters. The outer two layers filter waste chemicals from the blood. The waste trickles down microscopic tubes into the middle of the kidney, to form urine. This flows down a larger tube, the *ureter*, to the bladder.

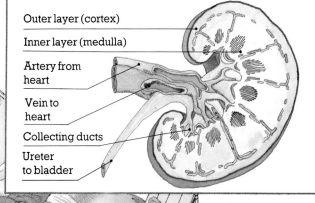

Outer layer (cortex)

Inner layer (medulla)

Artery from heart

Vein to heart

Collecting ducts

Ureter to bladder

Rectum

A useless organ?
Where your small and large intestines join is your appendix. This organ seems to have no use in the human body. Plant eaters like rabbits have a much bigger appendix which helps them digest tough plant food.

The end of the line
The "destruction line" has finished. Leftovers and waste wait to be removed in the *rectum*. The waste includes dead bacteria from the large intestine and rubbed-off bits of intestinal lining.

49

HOW YOU BEGAN

Every human being – and in fact every animal – begins life as one cell. This single cell contains all the instructions and information needed for a complete new animal to grow, develop, and live its life. If this information were written out in words, it would fill many books. But the information is in the form of microscopic chemical codes, packed inside the cell, which is smaller than a pinhead. This cell, the fertilized egg, is formed when a sperm cell from the father joins with an egg cell from the mother. At that moment, called *conception*, a new life begins.

How sperm are made
Sperm are made in a man's two *testes* (testicles). A continuous "production line" makes 500 million new sperm each day. They are stored in the *epididymis*, a long coiled tube. If they are not needed to fertilize an egg, they die and are absorbed by the body.

Where eggs come from
Eggs are stored in a woman's two ovaries. Each month an egg ripens and pops out of the ovary into the *Fallopian tube*, or egg tube. The womb's lining becomes thick with blood. If the egg is not fertilized, the lining comes away and passes out through the vagina. This is called *menstruation*.

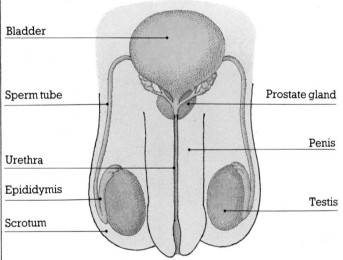

Bladder

Sperm tube

Prostate gland

Penis

Urethra

Epididymis

Testis

Scrotum

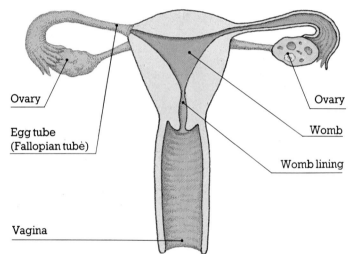

Ovary

Ovary

Egg tube (Fallopian tube)

Womb

Womb lining

Vagina

How a baby is conceived
A baby starts to develop when a woman's egg cell and a man's sperm cell join together. As the couple kiss and caress each other, the man's penis becomes larger and stiff, or "erect," and the woman's vagina becomes firmer. The man slides his penis into the woman's vagina and the muscles around his urethra contract, sending out about 300 million sperm in a milky liquid called semen. Like tadpoles, sperm have long tails to help them swim. They find the entrance to the womb and swim up through it into the egg tubes. The egg cell gives off a chemical that works like a homing device, helping the sperm to find the way. Once a surviving sperm reaches the egg, it will penetrate the outer membrane and fertilize it.

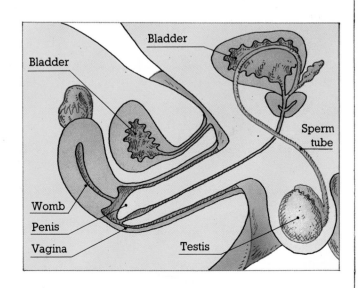

Bladder

Bladder

Sperm tube

Womb

Penis

Vagina

Testis

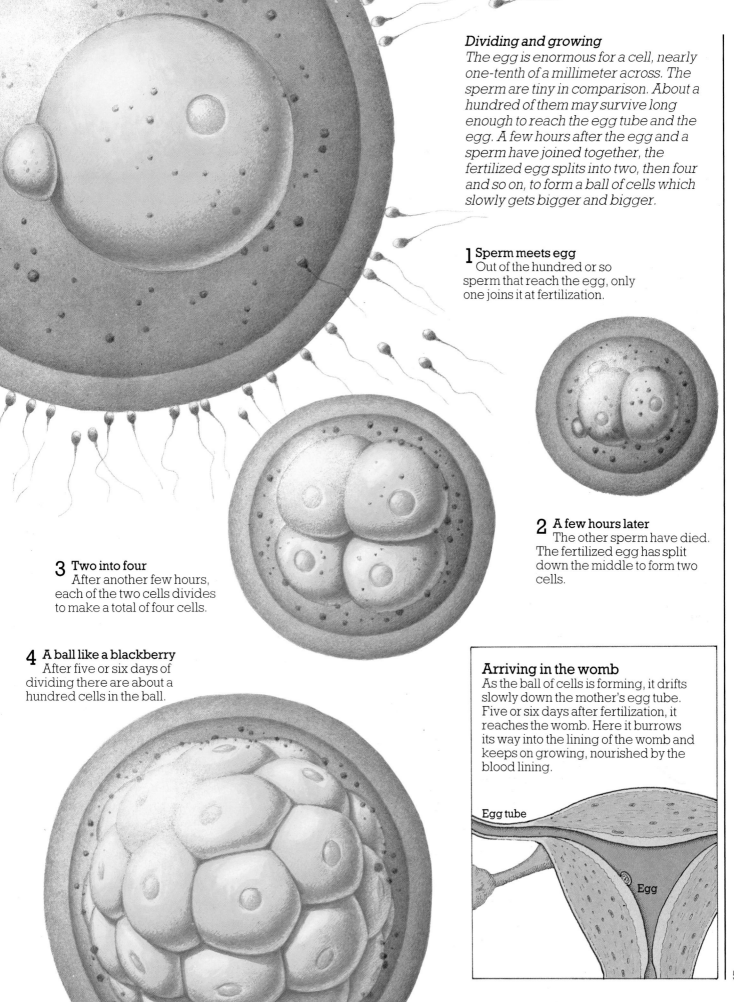

Dividing and growing

The egg is enormous for a cell, nearly one-tenth of a millimeter across. The sperm are tiny in comparison. About a hundred of them may survive long enough to reach the egg tube and the egg. A few hours after the egg and a sperm have joined together, the fertilized egg splits into two, then four and so on, to form a ball of cells which slowly gets bigger and bigger.

1 Sperm meets egg
Out of the hundred or so sperm that reach the egg, only one joins it at fertilization.

2 A few hours later
The other sperm have died. The fertilized egg has split down the middle to form two cells.

3 Two into four
After another few hours, each of the two cells divides to make a total of four cells.

4 A ball like a blackberry
After five or six days of dividing there are about a hundred cells in the ball.

Arriving in the womb

As the ball of cells is forming, it drifts slowly down the mother's egg tube. Five or six days after fertilization, it reaches the womb. Here it burrows its way into the lining of the womb and keeps on growing, nourished by the blood lining.

Egg tube

Egg

BEFORE YOU WERE BORN

At the very beginning of your life, you lived in your mother's womb. At first you were as small as a tiny dot, but your body grew and changed so much that after nine months of being in the womb you were ready to live in the outside world.

When you were in the womb, you lived inside a warm, safe bag full of watery liquid. You didn't eat through your mouth or breathe through your nose. You got all the air and food you needed from your mother's blood by means of a special tube attached at one end to your mother and at the other end to your stomach (*see page 55*).

After about three months in the womb you were able to move around, suck your thumb, and even turn somersaults. You slept a lot of the time, but when you were awake you could hear your mother's voice, the thumping of her heart, and the sound of food passing through her body.

After about nine months you were ready to be born.

Whose baby?

At the very beginning of your life in the womb you looked like other baby animals. It was several weeks before you began to look like a human baby.

Human Fetus	Rabbit Fetus	Lizard Fetus
3 weeks	1½ weeks	1 week
5 weeks	2 weeks	2 weeks
6 weeks	2½ weeks	3 weeks
8 weeks	3 weeks	4 weeks

The first nine months
Although you started life looking no bigger than a small dot, you soon began to look like a human baby. While babies are developing (before birth) they are called fetuses. In your mother's womb, you practiced a number of things that would help you after you were born. The most important of these were sucking and swallowing. This meant you could take milk from your mother's breast or from a baby's bottle as soon as you were born. You also learned to grip with your fingers, cough, sneeze, yawn, hiccup, and stretch.

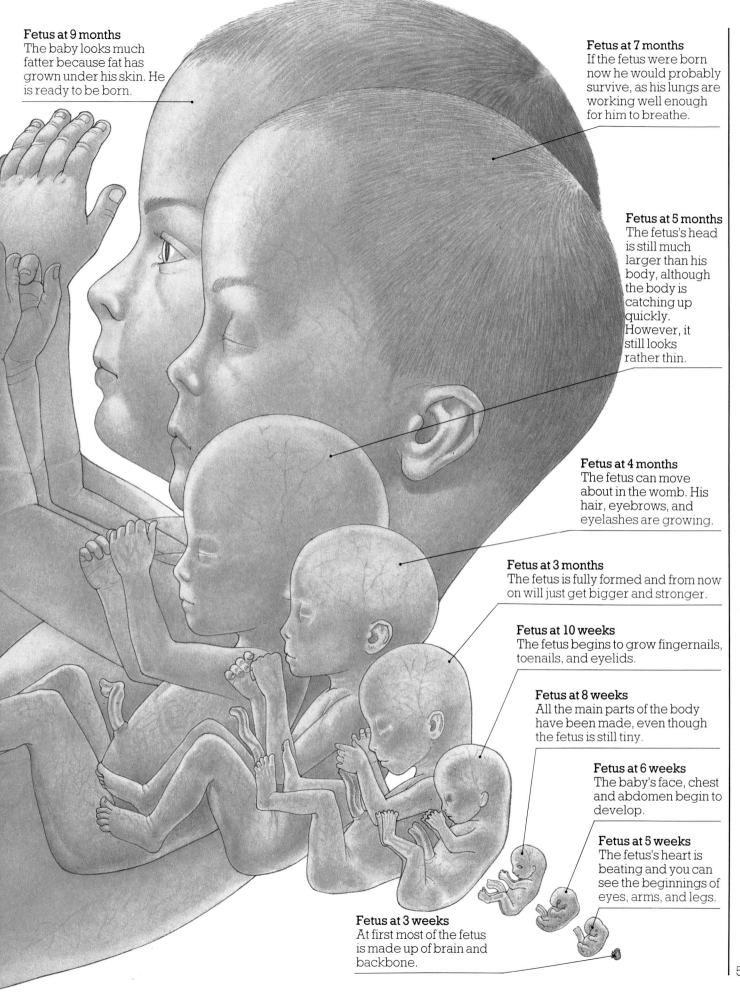

Fetus at 9 months
The baby looks much fatter because fat has grown under his skin. He is ready to be born.

Fetus at 7 months
If the fetus were born now he would probably survive, as his lungs are working well enough for him to breathe.

Fetus at 5 months
The fetus's head is still much larger than his body, although the body is catching up quickly. However, it still looks rather thin.

Fetus at 4 months
The fetus can move about in the womb. His hair, eyebrows, and eyelashes are growing.

Fetus at 3 months
The fetus is fully formed and from now on will just get bigger and stronger.

Fetus at 10 weeks
The fetus begins to grow fingernails, toenails, and eyelids.

Fetus at 8 weeks
All the main parts of the body have been made, even though the fetus is still tiny.

Fetus at 6 weeks
The baby's face, chest and abdomen begin to develop.

Fetus at 5 weeks
The fetus's heart is beating and you can see the beginnings of eyes, arms, and legs.

Fetus at 3 weeks
At first most of the fetus is made up of brain and backbone.

YOUR FIRST JOURNEY

Your first journey was on your birth day. For nine months you were in your mother's womb, where it was dark, quiet, and warm, floating in watery liquid. Then, on your birth day, the muscles in the womb wall squeezed – gently at first, then very strongly. The opening, or neck, of the womb became bigger and you were pushed out, little by little, along the birth canal. After a few hours of hard work by both you and your mother, you were born. You came out into a world that was bright and busy. You felt air on your skin and heard sounds all around. In a few seconds you had taken your first breaths, and soon you were sucking milk for your first meal. You looked and listened, but everything was strange and new. From that first day you began to learn about the world around you.

The way out of the womb

The pictures show how you gradually came out of the womb. The opening to the womb had been tightly shut for nine months, to hold in the watery liquid and protect you from germs. At birth it had to open wide enough to let through your biggest part, your head.

Leaving the womb

Before you were born you felt the womb tightly all around you (1). You were probably ready to be born head-first, like most babies. The opening of the womb became soft and loose, while the walls of the womb began to squeeze strongly. Your head was gradually pushed out of the womb (2). As the womb kept on pushing, your head turned (3), to pass through the large hole in the middle of your mother's hipbone. Gradually your head came out (4), then your body – and you were born.

How other animals are born

Different animals are born in different ways. Dogs and many other mammals are born in the same way as human babies. When a baby kangaroo is born it is tiny and has no fur. It crawls to its mother's pocket or "pouch," and stays there as it grows. The babies of the platypus grow and develop in eggs that their mother lays. Then they hatch out of the eggs, like birds. All the babies shown here are mammals and feed on their mothers' milk.

Dalmatian dog with her puppies

Kangaroo with her baby in her pouch

Platypus with her eggs

Helping you to breathe and feed
On the inside of the womb there was a network of blood cells called the *placenta*. It was the link between you and your mother. In the womb you did not have the same blood as your mother – you had your own, separate supply. Your blood flowed from your body along the *umbilical cord* to the placenta and back again. In the placenta, oxygen and digested food from your mother's blood passed into your blood. This was the way you breathed and fed.

Placenta

4

Umbilical
cord

Little room
in the womb

The aquarium
The liquid in your mother's womb helped to protect you from bumps before you were born. It also kept you at an even temperature and allowed you to grow and move about freely.

This is where you were just before you were born. You took up a lot of space in your mother's body.

PARENT TO CHILD

Do you look like your mother or your father – or both? Most children look like their parents. You might have "your mother's eyes" or "your father's nose." Your parents, in turn, look similar to their parents, and your children will resemble you. The passing of family likeness from parents to children is called *heredity*. Yet no two people look exactly the same, unless they are "identical twins." Each of us is different. Why is this?

A baby grows from a fertilized egg, which contains all the instructions needed for a new human being to live and grow (*see page 50*). The instructions are called *genes* and there are many thousands of them. They control much of what a person looks like: the color of his hair, skin, and eyes, the shape of his nose, and so on. Often many genes combine to determine a feature. There are two sets of genes. One set is inherited from the mother, in the egg, and the other set comes from the father, in the sperm. As a new baby grows, the mother's genes control some features while the father's genes are in charge of others. If a feature is controlled by many genes, they can form different combinations of the mother's and father's genes.

The "mixing and matching" of genes happens quite by chance. It explains why you look similar to your parents, but not exactly the same as them.

From grandparent to grandchild
Can you see the similarities between these people? The two below are grandparents. The woman to the right is their daughter, and her husband is next to her. The two youngest ones are the grandchildren.

Fair or red?
Hair color can change through life. Some people dye their hair. In others it is lightened by the sun, or it gradually goes gray with age. But hair's natural color is controlled by genes inherited from mother and father.

The grandmother below has passed her fair hair on to the mother. The father brought red hair into the family. The son has inherited red hair from his father, while the daughter has inherited fair hair from her mother.

Boy or girl?

Whether you are a boy or girl depends on the genes found on tiny *chromosomes*. There are 23 chromosomes in an egg and 23 in a sperm. One of the 23 is the sex chromosome. The egg's sex chromosome is always X. The sperm's can be X or Y. When an X-carrying sperm joins an egg, the fertilized egg has two X chromosomes. XX is the code for a girl. With a Y-carrying sperm, the result is XY, the code for a boy. About half the sperm carry an X chromosome and half a Y chromosome, so half the children born are girls and the other half boys.

Father XY   Mother XX

Sperm   Sperm   Egg   Egg

X   Y   X   X

Girl XX   Boy XY   Girl XX   Boy XY

Family groups

Humans are like one big family. Apart from different shades of skin, hair, and eyes, and different body sizes, we all look basically the same. All the people in the world belong to the same group, or *species*. It's the same for other animals. All horses look much the same and belong to the horse species. Zebras form a species of their own.

Blue or brown?

Eye color is passed from parent to child. Like other features, there are two genes controlling it – one from the mother and one from the father. But in this case the two genes are not the same strength.

A "brown" gene, giving brown eyes, is stronger than a "blue" gene. In the family below, each grandparent has blue eyes, because they each have two "blue" genes. The mother has inherited "blue" genes, so she has blue eyes. The father has "blue" and "brown" genes. His eyes are brown. Their son has two "blue" genes, but their daughter has inherited her father's "brown" genes.

It runs in the family

The son in the picture below has inherited his "grandmother's nose." This means that his nose is the same shape as hers. He can pass on the genes which determine this nose to future generations.

THE CHANGING BODY

Throughout life, the human body changes in size and shape. It starts as a tiny speck called a fertilized egg. In nine months this grows into a baby, ready to be born (*see pages 51-53*). After birth we can see the changes as a baby grows. In the beginning, these happen very quickly. During childhood the body is still growing, but the speed of growth gradually slows down. As a person reaches adulthood, at about 20 years of age, growth stops.

No one understands how the body "knows" when to stop growing. It may be that some cells in the body have "clocks" in them that count the number of times they divide. (More cells mean a bigger body.) Perhaps when the number of divisions reaches a certain amount, the cells stop dividing, and growth stops.

Between about 20 and 50 years of age, the body does not change much in outward appearance. Yet there is always activity inside. Nutrients in food are used to build new tissues to replace worn-out ones. As old age approaches, the body cannot repair the wear and tear so quickly. Parts may malfunction, and people are more likely to fall ill. But people who take care of their bodies when they are young can stay healthy well into old age.

Chemicals in control

Going around your body, in your blood, are chemicals called *hormones*. There are over 20 different hormones, and each one controls a particular process. Some of these processes take years, such as growing up. Others go on all the time, such as adjusting the amounts of water and salt in your body.

Hormones are made in special glands called endocrine glands. Your adrenal glands, lying on top of your kidneys, make the hormone adrenaline. When you get excited or frightened, adrenaline is released into your bloodstream. Adrenaline makes your heart beat faster, your skin get sweaty, and your lungs breathe more quickly, preparing your body for action.

Sex hormones from the ovaries control the cycle of egg release in women. In men, sex hormones from the testes control sperm production. Insulin, a hormone from the pancreas, controls the amount of sugar in your blood.

From small to tall

As a person grows, not all the parts of his body grow bigger at the same rate. A baby has a large head and body in proportion to his short arms and legs. Over the years his head grows only a little. His body grows slightly faster. His arms grow even faster, and his legs grow fastest of all. By the time he is grown up, his head and body are quite small in proportion to his long arms and legs.

Who lives longest?

Compared to most other animals, humans have a long life. In general, the bigger an animal is, the longer it lives, as you can see below. Small creatures like insects, spiders, and snails live only a few years on average. Some of the animals who live the longest are large reptiles like giant tortoises and crocodiles.

Mouse: 9 months-1 year

Cat: 13-17 years

Elephant: 20-30 years

Giant tortoise: about 50 years

Human: 70-75 years

1 year old

At this age, most babies are just beginning to learn to walk. The average baby is about 30 in (75 cm) and weighs about 22 lb (10 kg). Boys are often slightly taller and heavier than girls. A baby does not have to be chubby to be healthy.

6 years old

The average six-year-old is about 4 ft (1.2 m) tall and weighs about 55 lb (25 kg). He is growing about 2 in (5 cm) taller and 5 or 6 lb (2.5 kg) heavier each year. He has already learned to walk, talk, run, throw, read, and write.

14 years old
This is the time of puberty, when many body changes occur. Boys have suddenly started growing more quickly – more than 3 in (8 cm) a year for three years or so. Girls do the same, but their growth spurt starts when they are about eleven or twelve.

20 years old
Most people are fully grown by this age, at least in their height. Men average 5 ft, 8 in (1.74 m) in height; and women 5 ft, 3 in (1.61 m). Weight tends to vary much more depending on diet and heredity. The muscles are still continuing to develop.

45-50 years old
During middle age, there are few outward changes in the body. Some people may put on a little weight. Some men also start to lose their hair from the top of their head. A few wrinkles may appear in the skin, especially for people living in sunny places.

60-70 years old
The skin gradually becomes more wrinkled. And most people become shorter, so they are 2 to 3 in (about 6 cm) smaller than at the age of 20. This is because the discs between the bones in the back shrink, as do the muscles that help them stand upright.

LEGS AND FEET

Your arms and your legs are built from the same basic parts (*see page 19*). There are about the same number of bones and muscles in each. Your thigh, like your upper arm, has one long bone. Your calf, like your forearm, has two long bones. Your knee joint is similar to your elbow joint. But there are many small differences in the sizes and shapes of the parts. These add up to make your legs longer, stronger, and less flexible than your arms. While arms are suited to reaching and holding, legs are designed to carry the weight of your body and let you walk, run, and jump. Your leg muscles are among the biggest and strongest in your body. When you run, they need lots of oxygen and energy, so you have to breathe fast and deep. Your heart works hard to pump more blood to them.

Levers for walking
Like your arm, your leg is a double lever. In fact, your foot acts as a short third lever, as you bend your ankle and push against the ground with the ball of your foot and toes when you walk or run.

Longest and strongest
Your thighbone is the longest and strongest bone in your body. At the top its ball-shaped end fits snugly into a socket in your hipbone. Five strong straps called ligaments hold your hipbone and thighbone together. Your hip joint is very strong, but it cannot move as freely as your shoulder joint.

Your largest joint
Your knee is the largest joint in your body. It is protected at the front by a small triangular bone, your kneecap. Your knees "lock" firmly when you stand with your legs straight. This means you use less muscle power, so standing is not too tiring.

The elastic foot
Like your wrist and hand, your ankle and foot are made of many bones: 26 in all. The foot bones form an elastic arch that flattens when you put your foot down and springs back to a curved shape when you lift it.

Jumping with joints
Each joint in your leg is different. Your hip is a *ball-and-socket* joint. It can move in any direction, like the joint at the bottom of a computer joystick. Your knee is a *hinge* joint, like the hinge on a door. It can swing forward and backward, but not sideways. Your ankle is a *sliding* joint. Each ankle bone moves only a little, but the whole ankle is quite flexible. In general, the more directions a joint can move in, the weaker it is. Less movement means more strength. The knee is extremely strong but not very flexible. The shoulder is very flexible but not particularly strong, and sometimes the bones slip or "dislocate."

Ball-and-socket joint in hip

Hinge joint in knee

Sliding joint in ankle

Thigh muscles
The large, powerful muscles in your upper thigh bend, straighten, and twist your hip. Muscles in your lower thigh bend and straighten your knee.

Calf muscles
These muscles mainly bend, straighten, and twist your ankle. If someone stands up straight and rocks to and fro, you can see his calf muscles moving.

Ankle strapping
Long, rope-like *tendons* connect your calf muscles to your ankle and foot bones. They slide under strong strap-like ligaments that strengthen your ankle.

Ankle bones?
The hard, knobby parts of your ankle are not ankle bones, but the ends of the long bones in your lower leg.

Leathery soles
The sole of your foot is covered with the thickest skin on your body. If you do not wear shoes for a while, it becomes even thicker – your own leathery sole.

The length of the legs
Even though humans have only two legs, these are long and let us move quite fast. A good runner can sprint at over 15 miles (30 km) per hour. Animals that use all four legs usually go even faster. A rhinoceros has stumpy legs to support its enormous weight, but it can run almost as fast as a human over short distances. The cheetah has a top speed of over 60 miles (100 km) per hour. It has very long, light legs and a slim body. As the cheetah runs, its back arches up and down, to increase the stretch of its legs.

Rhinoceros

Cheetah

GLOSSARY

The words in *italics* have their own entries in the glossary.

alveoli (singular: **alveolus**)
The tiny "bubbles" inside your lungs that fill with air as you breathe in.

atrium (plural: **atria**)
The upper chamber on each side of your heart.

bronchi (singular: **bronchus**)
The air tubes that join your lungs and the main air tube, your *trachea*.

capillaries
The microscopic tubes that carry blood to every *cell* of your body.

cells
The tiny living units that make up your body.

cerebral cortexes
The two main areas of your brain.

chromosomes
The thread-like parts inside the nucleus of each *cell* that carry the genes.

cochlea
A snail-shaped tube that forms part of your inner ear.

cornea
The transparent tissue at the front of the colored part of your eye.

cranium
The upper part of your skull.

dendrites
The "fingers" of your nerve cells along which each *cell* can send signals to other nerve cells.

dermis
The lower layer of your skin, immediately beneath the *epidermis*.

diaphragm
The dome-shaped muscle, used in breathing, just beneath your lungs.

duodenum
The first part of your small intestine, where digestive juices dissolve food into tiny pieces.

epidermis
The outer layer of your skin.

esophagus
The muscular tube joining the back of your throat to your stomach.

Eustachian tube
The narrow tube joining your ear to the back of your throat.

Fallopian tubes
The two tubes joining a woman's ovaries to her womb.

fetus
An unborn, developing baby.

follicles
Deep pits in your skin, from which hair grows.

genes
The coded instructions, inherited from your parents, that determine your looks and characteristics.

heredity
The passing on of family likeness and characteristics through coded instructions called *genes*.

hormones
Chemicals that control your body's growth and development.

iris
The colored part of your eye.

keratin
The hard substance from which fingernails, claws, horns, and hooves are made.

ligaments
Strong, strap-like fibers that hold your bones together.

marrow
The jelly-like substance inside your bones that makes all of your red blood cells and some of your white blood cells.

melanin
The coloring substance found in skin which can darken it and protect it from sun damage.

motor nerves
The nerves that carry instructions from the brain to the muscles.

myelin sheath
The fatty covering of the nerve fiber, along which signals are passed.

neurons
Another name for nerve cells.

periosteum
The living "outer skin" or outer layer of your bones.

peristalsis
The "traveling wave," or muscular action, that pushes food down your esophagus and through your entire digestive system.

plasma
The watery liquid that carries your blood cells and contains dissolved chemicals, such as salt.

platelets
Tiny fragments of *cells* in your blood that help it to clot.

rectum
The last part of your large intestine, in which waste is stored before it leaves your body.

reflex
An involuntary movement made by one of your muscles.

retina
The innermost layer of tissue at the back of your eyeball.

sacrum
The wedge-shaped bone at the bottom of your backbone.

sebaceous glands
Tiny glands in your skin that make "natural oils" to prevent it from drying out and cracking.

sensory nerves
The nerves that carry information from your sense organs to your brain.

tendons
The fibers that hold your muscles to your bones.

thalamus
The part of your brain that sorts out signals from your sense organs and redirects them to the appropriate area of the brain.

trachea
Your windpipe; the main air tube that connects your lungs to your throat.

ventricle
The lower chamber on each side of your heart.

vertebrae (singular: **vertebra**)
The separate bones of your backbone.

INDEX

INDEX